OVERNIGHT SUCCESS

THE INNER GAME PLAYBOOK
FOR YOUR FIRST
BIG BREAKTHROUGH

JARED A. GOETZ

Typesetting and formatting by access ideas

ISBN: 9781795341448

Contents

Preface

My guess is you picked up this book with one question on your mind: "Is overnight success really possible?" I'm here to tell you *it is*. What I'm about to share with you has the power to instantly change your life for the better .

Your life is not the result of fate. You aren't where you are right now because of the economy, the government, your parents, your friends, your level of formal education or your IQ. You are where you are right now because of your decisions, and the only way to change your life is to *make different decisions than you've made in the past* .

Everyone on this earth has the ability to succeed. We all face different obstacles. On the surface, it might look like some people have it easier than others. But life is not just a surface level journey. It is also an inward journey.

The inward battle all of us fight every day is what determines our trajectory through life. Our inner game influences our decisions, and our decisions are what lead us to experience either massive breakthroughs or painful defeats.

No one likes to lose! That's for sure. But the good news is that by mastering your inner game, it's possible to completely eliminate "failure" from your life.

When you eliminate failure from your life, that doesn't mean you always get what you want. It doesn't mean everything always turns out exactly as planned. It doesn't mean you no longer experience frustration or setbacks.

When you eliminate failure from your life, what it really means is every experience you have that isn't what you wanted it to be, you now view as an opportunity to *make a new decision* .

Do you want to experience levels of joy, satisfaction, connection, and prosperity that you've never experienced before in your entire life? If you do, then now is probably the time to make a decision you've never made before.

I can't tell you what that decision is. I don't know the ins and outs of your personal journey. I don't know if success is going to knock on your door tomorrow, or if it will call on you in the middle of the night.

But I can tell you this: success is always the product of decision, and your success may be hanging out on the flip side of a very simple one you just haven't realized you need to make yet. *The moment you realize what that decision is and make it, success is yours.*

That's why I'm so excited and grateful for this opportunity to share my story with you in this book! You may be struggling and wondering when things are going to get better. If that's the case, I've been exactly where you are right now, as you will soon find out.

As you read the following pages, look for sentences and paragraphs that speak to you the most. Highlight or underline them so you don't forget their importance. Remember, one single idea in this book could change your entire life. So, if something you read inspires you to make a new decision you've never considered making before, put this book down, and take action immediately!

Don't be discouraged if it feels like your goals are way far off in the distance. I wrote this book to help you realize just how close they really are, all the time, no matter what it looks like. Because I truly believe if I can succeed in turning my life around when it looked like all was lost, not once, but multiple times, so can you!

Chapter 1

Everything is On the Menu for You

If I could give a younger version of myself one piece of advice, the advice contained in this first chapter would be it. It starts with this understanding—we all have standards and beliefs. These live in our subconscious minds. As we grow, try new things, and keep pushing ourselves; eventually, something finally clicks, our dreams start to fall into place, and these standards and beliefs start to shift upward.

When this happens, most of the time it surprises us. When you've been working hard and trying to achieve any kind of success in life, it's incredibly surreal to break through to the other side of the struggle—to the place where your mind says, "Okay, that was cool. I like where I'm at, but now what? How can I take this further?"

This point in life is attainable for you. You don't have to be special, gifted, or well-connected. You just have to keep pushing yourself until you actually get what you want. That's it.

Now, you might be thinking, "If it's so simple, why don't more people get what they want out of life?" Here's the reason why: they don't believe they can. They don't understand that their subconscious beliefs about who they are now, what they're capable of, and who they are meant to be are holding them back.

The amazing thing is all it takes is a small taste of success to completely shatter all of your subconscious limitations. A whole new and better life can be yours if you put in the work required to get what you want for long enough. You don't have to accept the standards and beliefs you were born into. You can change them. In fact, it's your job to change them if you want to build momentum, take control of your life, and succeed at a high level.

People are far more powerful and capable than they often lead themselves to believe. We tend to think of ourselves as average, and by default, that everyone else who is successful in life is some kind of genius.

But I'm going to share with you my story and how I went from being flat broke, depressed, and stressed out, to owning a business that did almost $5 million in sales in its first year, and went on to create multiple seven- and eight-figure businesses thereafter. That's just the tip of the iceberg of what I now believe is possible, but I didn't have this kind of confidence in the beginning.

I grew up with a single mother in a one-bedroom apartment in New York. I watched my mom work two jobs to make sure we always had everything we needed. We were middle-class, and we were always fine, but I knew things weren't easy for my mom.

From a young age, I was conscious of the importance of money. I saw other people who owned successful businesses, and I wanted to be in business for myself someday. But deep down inside, I questioned myself. I wasn't sure if I had it in me.

Like most people, I had no reason to believe I was anybody special. I knew succeeding in business was possible in theory and wanted to do it, but my mental conditioning didn't allow me to own the possibility until I could see it in the flesh.

For example, growing up, when we went out to eat, I was taught to pick out what I was going to order based off the price of the food on the menu. You don't order steak when money is a concern. Too expensive. You order chicken. You don't order a Coke. You get a glass of ice water.

Please don't misunderstand me. I'm not at all complaining about the way I was raised. I learned a lot of important things about life growing up, but what I learned was not everything I needed to know to take myself from where I was to where I wanted to be in terms of income, business success, and personal freedom.

Was ordering or not ordering steak at a restaurant going to put my family's finances in jeopardy or make us any wealthier? No. This is just a small example of the real, bigger problem. It's small things like this that can sneak into your subconscious mind and drive your life in the opposite direction of where you truly want to go, without you even knowing it.

When you look at a restaurant menu, and you start categorizing all the stuff you actually want to get as "too expensive," what you're doing is putting limits on yourself. Even as we mature in life, these limits sometimes stick with us. You can be earning $200,000 a year and still feel guilty, and not know why, when you order steak at restaurant. It might just feel "wrong" to you. That's your subconscious mind talking to you, and it can be your best friend or your worst enemy.

The subconscious mind has a set range of what it considers possible and acceptable. When we drop below this range, we start to freak out. When we go above it too fast, we start to question ourselves and wonder if we're taking on too much risk. This is not a bad thing.

We need our subconscious to keep us in balance. We need to know when to take risk and when to dial things back. The problem is that without knowing the subconscious has this role, we either bite off more than we can chew, or we don't try nearly hard enough to get what we want.

Let me tell you about a time when I bit off more than I could chew. When I turned twenty years old, I was ambitious, hungry, and naïve. I didn't want to let my subconscious beliefs hold me back at all. I wanted to succeed in business, so I started a concert promotion company.

It was a huge success, and by the time I was twenty-one, I had made almost a million dollars. Gone were the middle-class standards I had grown up with. My ego skyrocketed, and I wasn't at all content with what I had achieved. Instead, I decided I wanted to become the world's biggest concert promoter.

So I went from doing shows on college campuses all across the United States, to booking a massive arena tour and setting up the biggest show I had ever done to date. Unfortunately, I got in way over my head. The first show ended up costing me way more money to put on than I had anticipated, and we barely sold any tickets.

Then, just like that, *I lost all my money in one night.*

Suddenly, my belief in myself collapsed. Success, money, and the good life I wanted were now off the menu for me. I started to question myself and think, "Maybe owning my own business is not for me. Maybe I'm not smart enough. Maybe I could succeed if I had the backing of a wealthy family, but I don't."

I again wondered if it was even possible for someone like me to succeed at a high level. I started to believe a lot of the same stories most people believe–that being successful, making money, and owning a profitable business is all about getting lucky, and that only people who are "special" can do it.

I started to undervalue myself. I didn't know how to code. I didn't know how to build apps or social media sites or anything like that. I looked at all the things I couldn't do, instead of looking at all the skills I did have that had gotten me to the point of being able to book an arena show in the first place.

This is what a lot of people do when they experience failure in life. They start to assume they're failures in every way instead of looking at their failure as something they can learn from.

After this incident, it took me a few years to get back into a good state of mind. When you're down like I was, it's almost impossible to see any kind of opportunity in front of you. Fortunately, my previous concert promotion success did not go unnoticed by other people. My shows were actually pretty well-known all throughout the country.

Because of my previous success, a start-up company reached out to me to see if I could help them grow their social media app, which they were trying to market to college students, the same demographic I had a lot of experience promoting my events to.

When they contacted me, they had no idea my event company didn't exist anymore, but I was honest with them about how it had failed. I was also honest with them about what I thought the best way to market their app was.

I advised them to use a similar marketing tactic to the one I had used to sell out shows on college campuses, night after night. Seeing the value my experience could bring their company, the start-up hired me to work for them.

Just after I came on board with the company, they were able to raise another $60 million to add to their initial seed investment of $10 million, and my shares of the company went up fifteen times what they were initially worth. But the real benefit of being hired was that my state of mind improved drastically.

I was able to get some perspective on my whole situation, and I could finally see it wasn't all over for me. Once again, my subconscious standards rose to a higher level, and the world didn't look so devoid of opportunity anymore. I started to believe in myself again, and I started to appreciate my failure for what it had taught me about myself, about life, and about business. With my mind in a better place after I was hired to work at the start-up company, I started to take on what I call an opportunistic viewpoint.

When you're operating with low energy, and you're depressed and in a rut, you don't see opportunities. When you feel like shit, all you see are shitty opportunities, and you just want to give up. But when you feel good and have an opportunistic viewpoint, you see good opportunities, and you're able to act on them.

The first good opportunity I saw came to me when I got a hoverboard in my hands for the first time at a tradeshow I attended in China. I was actually one of the first people to ever see one of those things, and I immediately knew it was a product that had huge potential.

I knew I needed to act fast in order to be one of the first people to start selling hoverboards in America, so I immediately took action. In my first month, I sold $250,000 worth of hoverboards.

Once again, my standards and what I believed was possible in my life rose higher. At the time, I was used to making about $55,000 a year at my job, but the success I had selling hoverboards took me well beyond that and inspired me to keep pushing for more.

So, I went out to China again, and I started hunting for more viral products to sell. Since my confidence was up again, I was able to find another great product—an inflatable lounger—and, soon, making $2,000 a day was my new standard.

If I was making $2,000 a day, I was happy. If I was making $1,000 a day, I was concerned. If I was making $500 a day, I was very concerned. And if I was making $250 a day, which was what I was making at my job before I started importing products to sell myself, I was in panic mode.

My subconscious simply would not allow me to drop down any lower than the $250 panic mode, so I found myself living at a much higher level all the time. At this higher level, I started seeing opportunities everywhere. The new challenge became trying to decide what opportunities would not only bring me the most benefit in terms of profit but also what opportunities would fit best with my ultimate vision for what I want my life to be about.

I want what I do to bring value to people and help them. That's a major reason why I started an online course and community and why I'm writing this book.

When everything crashed and burned with my concert promotion business, I was lost. Before the crash, I had been living the life of a big-time concert promoter. I lived in a penthouse. I went out to Miami nightclubs as much as possible, bought bottles, and lived as high as I could. I had a good time, but the overall experience left me feeling unfulfilled.

After an intense period of reflection, I realized what I loved about putting on shows was never the money, success, or attention it brought me. It was being able to give people an unforgettable experience.

I didn't know what to do when I could no longer do that. When the bottom fell out, I had no money left to live. I went from believing I could grind my way into doing anything I wanted in life, to just wanting to reset completely. I went from grinding every day, 24/7, to barely being able to get myself out of bed.

The only thing I could think to do was go back to my mom's place in New York. I knew I needed to find myself again, so I decided to give myself a month to wake up early every morning, go for a run, read, meditate, and get back in touch with myself.

I didn't have much self-awareness back then. I didn't know how to be the best version of myself internally. I thought succeeding in life was all about grinding. That was how I defined myself, but when I didn't have the money or success to back this definition of myself up, I felt completely defeated.

Back at my mom's place, the first thing I started to do was exercise. I started waking up early every morning to go out and try to run off my depression. I ran as much as I could. I wasn't good at running, but I figured if I did it a little bit every day, it would help me. My mom lived in Freeport, New York, at the time, which is near the water.

So I'd go out and run and take a book with me to read. Most days, I would run to a bench that looked out over the water, and I'd just sit there and read. One of the books I read during this time was a book called *The Way of the Peaceful Warrior* by Dan Millman.

It's a fictional book, but it introduced me to a lot of things I knew nothing about back then. It served as my introduction to personal development, and the main character in it reminded me a lot of myself. The book is about a guy who thinks he's got everything in life figured out, only to realize he doesn't.

I could relate to this character on a deep level. On the one hand, I had achieved some incredible things by age twenty-one, but life was showing me I still had a lot to learn. Mainly, I needed to learn about balance.

Here's some advice you won't get from most entrepreneurs, influencers, or gurus. If you don't have balance in your life, you have nothing. Most entrepreneurs preach a different message. They say, "Work, work, work! 10X everything! Grind seven days a week, and never stop!"

There's some truth to the 10X rule. To succeed in business long-term, you have to work harder and care more about what you're doing than anybody else. The problem is you can't do this long-term unless you also take care of yourself.

If you don't take care of yourself, you're going to burn yourself out. So, if you want to 10X your business, start by going 10X on your own personal development. Reading this book from cover to cover is a great place to start with that.

If your business suddenly explodes, but you're not ready for it, it's going to be too much for you, and you'll end up needing a reset like I needed when my world crumbled around me. Focus on strengthening yourself from the inside out, and examine the subconscious standards that are driving you to either push forward or slow down.

Massive personal growth happens when your internal world matches your external world. When these two worlds are aligned, confidence is born, and from confidence comes momentum. When you have these two things carrying you forward and allowing you to outperform your own subconscious limiting beliefs, that's when you can truly become a force in business and in life. And everything is on the menu for you.

This book is going to walk you through everything I've learned on my journey from rock bottom to achieving everything I've ever wanted in life and then some. No matter where you're starting from or where you want to get to, success begins with the foundational principles we're going to talk about right here, so let's get started right now on this journey together!

Chapter 2

Feel Good, Do Good

Once I got my first big win in business, I started operating at a much higher level. I started seeing opportunities everywhere, and that's about the time I discovered drop-shipping. At first, it sounded too good to be true, but since I believed much more was possible, I was more willing to explore different things to see what could happen before making a judgment.

When I started drop-shipping, after putting in a good amount of work, I got my store up to the point where it was doing $2,000 a day in revenue. I was excited about this, but I also intuitively knew so much more was possible. I knew if $2,000 a day was possible with the amount of work I'd put in, by trying and testing new ideas, I could potentially blow this out of the water.

I was excited about this new success I had had with drop-shipping as I headed out to a Tony Robbins event called UPW in LA. After the event, I had to drive all the way across the country from LA to South Florida, where I was moving to at the time. This meant I had to drive twelve to eighteen hours a day for five days straight.

During this fateful drive, I had a lot of time to reflect and process what was going on in my life and business. My mind was relaxed and in a good place after spending the last few days in a very positive environment surrounded by people who inspired me, and I began to notice creativity was flowing through me like never before.

At this point in time, I had two people helping me run my drop-shipping business. I had a media buyer who was helping me with my advertising, and I had a virtual assistant who was helping me with customer support, answering emails, and making sure my customers were taken care of if they had any issues.

During my drive, my mind was focused on my business. I kept thinking of new ideas for how to scale, how to put new systems in place, and how to take my business to the next level. When my mind landed upon an idea that felt like a good one worth testing, I sent it out to my media buyer and virtual assistant.

Many of the ideas I thought of worked out *better* than I anticipated. Over the course of this drive, my business went from doing $2,000 a day to doing $50,000 a day in revenue in just five days. My mind was blown, and my standards skyrocketed to the point where if I wasn't profiting at least $10,000 a day, I felt like something was wrong.

Everyone has standards. We're born with them, and our childhood and life experiences create and cement them in our minds. Most people simply accept the standards they start out with as the level their life is going to stay at, no matter what. But it doesn't have to be this way.

You can outwork your standards. You can outwork yourself. However, unless you push yourself and try new things until something works for you, you are going to continue to produce the same results in every area of your life, year after year.

The good news is that all it takes is one experience, one realization of something that formerly felt impossible, to totally demolish your former standards and raise the bar in your life higher than you ever imagined.

I'm at the point right now where I'm pushing myself to reach $500,000 a day in revenue across all of my businesses. I know, without a doubt, I can get there, but ten years ago, there's no way I would have ever set a goal this high. My belief in myself has compounded over time, and yours can too. It is up to you whether your belief in yourself trends in a positive direction or a negative one. That's why knowing which way your momentum is taking you is so important.

You can create negative momentum in your life, or you can create positive momentum. Both begin in the mind and are created by the way you choose to see the world and interact with it.

As I've gone about teaching others all I know about e-commerce for the last few years, it's become very easy for me to spot students who I know will succeed, and students who I know will fail unless they turn things around and commit to building positive momentum.

For example, when someone makes a post looking for help in our community support group, I can instantly tell where their head is. Every one of us faces challenges when we're getting started in business, but how we respond to these challenges determines the results we ultimately get.

If someone posts about a small problem they are having with their website, there are two ways this can go. The positive way is when my team and I respond, help the person troubleshoot the issue, and then they are able to correct it with a little bit of effort.

The negative way is when someone posts about a problem, gets frustrated that the issue takes time to troubleshoot, and then allows themselves to become even more frustrated than before—not just with the issue itself, but also with the fact that they have to spend time correcting it!

This is the effect of compounding frustration. It makes things worse than they really are in your mind. And you can bet, when you allow small problems like a little piece of troublesome code on your website to push you beyond your limits, you are going to get flattened when more serious issues pop up in your business.

I'm not saying small problems aren't frustrating, or that they can be ignored. But allowing yourself to become emotionally attached to small problems is first going to slow you down, and then will eventually bring you to a complete halt.

Attaching your emotions to small problems is a recipe for disaster and unnecessary stress. It leads you to believing things like, "Running my own business causes nothing but problems. I've tried my best, but it's just not worth it to keep going."

When you start thinking this way, negative momentum takes control, and negative momentum always leads to the path of least resistance. In today's world, the path of least resistance is Netflix, Instagram, Facebook, and the act of passively living through other people's lives you find more exciting than your own.

This is why you cannot let problems affect your psyche. The path of least resistance is the most dangerous one to travel for an entrepreneur, and it is the default path for those who don't know how to control their emotions and look at the big picture in moments of stress.

You have to recognize that, although the odds may not be in your favor right now, the only path to success is to keep trying. Eventually, if you don't give up, you will hit that one in one hundred or one in one thousand chance. And once you do that, the odds finally start to swing in your favor every time you take another shot.

When you're just getting started, you have to remember if you try one thousand things, one will work. But if you get discouraged and start focusing on small, unimportant issues after only one or two tries, that's it. It's game over.

Most of the time, we are way closer to a big win than we can see with our own eyes. If you're trying, even if you haven't seen any significant success, you are close—*much closer than everyone else who has already given up.*

So, what can you do to produce high-quality energy in your life and keep yourself moving forward, no matter what? How do you build positive energy and momentum in your life to the point where small problems no longer bother you? How can you make yourself comfortable with the very real possibility that you're going to have to "fail" your way to success?

All I can do is speak from my real-world experience on this because experience is the best teacher of the truth. In order for me to protect and create positive energy in my life, I absolutely have to start my day in a way that is most beneficial for me.

For example, if I allow myself to sleep in and wake up at 8:00 a.m., the first thought that's going to go through mind when I wake up is, "I'm fucked today." Not a good thought to start a productive day with, I'm sure you would agree.

So, I know I need to be up at about 4:30 a.m. for my day to be good. I find myself becoming more and more anxious throughout the day if I don't reserve time to center and ground myself first thing every morning.

I don't want my whole world coming down on me while I'm still half asleep. That's why I try to get up and be proactive about my day before anyone else can interrupt it. At 8:00 a.m., I know people are going to be trying to get a hold of me, wanting me to take a look at different things, and expecting me to be ready to perform at a high level. I can't do that if I'm just rolling out of bed. That's just not how I operate.

I like to ease into my day. Every morning, I go out into my living room and I spend some time writing down whatever is on my mind. I have a cup of coffee, and then I do some stretches. From there, I intentionally do the things I know I have to do to put myself into a peak mindset.

I go out for a run, or I go to the gym. This increases my energy. When I have increased energy for the day, I can see opportunities I might otherwise miss. I can also problem solve much better.

A positive, energetic mindset allows solutions to flow into small problems before they grow into massive ones, and when you can knock problems out like flies, you can actually get some enjoyment out of dealing with them most of the time.

But if you have a bad mindset, or you're tired, or you just haven't done anything to prepare for your day, that's like trying to win a footrace starting from twenty feet behind everybody else. If you're extremely fast, you might be able to make up the difference. But even if you do, you're going to have to work much harder, and you will exhaust yourself in the process.

If you have a bad mindset, everyday success can only be achieved through a lot of forced effort—this means the only things you'll get done are the things you absolutely have to do. This leaves no room for creativity or opportunity because all of your headspace must go towards the process of dealing with obligations, mission-critical worries, and looming deadlines.

You can see why this is a horrible mindset for any entrepreneur to live within. The only thing it's responsible for producing is the silent killer we have politely named *stress*.

A positive mindset produces the exact opposite. A positive mindset produces opportunity, deeper conversations

15

with team members and people in your network, financial abundance, peace of mind, fulfillment, and happiness. When you are feeling confident and strong, you also leave stronger impressions on people.

Knowing all of this, doesn't it make sense to do absolutely everything you can to make sure you are living every day with a positive mindset, ready to perform at the highest level? To me, there is no question: anything you can do to increase your sense of well-being, you should do!

Keeping that in mind, I'm about to give you some advice that goes against everything your financial advisor, society, or your parents might have taught you about money. The average person does not understand the power of making indirect investments with money. Since they don't understand this concept, this is why we often see rich people stereotyped as wasteful, extravagant, or even "evil."

Society sometimes scoffs at the man they see driving down the road in a luxury or exotic car. They think he must have cheated somebody out of their money to get it. They don't see the hours, days, weeks, months, and years of blood, sweat, and tears he endured to get that car. Even if they do begin to grasp the hard work it took to get the car, they still might say to themselves, "What a waste! Other people could use that money for something better!"

They say this because they don't understand what it takes to succeed at a high level. They don't understand what it takes for a human being to stretch themselves beyond their limits and try every day to bring something positive and good into the world that other people can enjoy.

It takes everything you've got to be a truly successful entrepreneur. This is why indirect investments are critical to your success at all levels of the game. As you grow and develop as an individual, the indirect investments you make in yourself should grow in proportion to the size of the impact you want to make on the world.

So, first of all, what is an indirect investment? An indirect investment is anything you buy for yourself or your family that is purely for personal enjoyment and which doesn't necessarily make you money in return. Indirect investments return emotional value and lead to a higher personal-peak mindset.

For example, if you go out and buy a Lamborghini, any financial advisor is going to tell you you're stupid. But when you drive that Lamborghini, if it makes you feel like you can do incredible things, that is going to impact how you live your life, what you do, and what you don't do.

The way you feel affects the choices you make, be they positive or negative, and the choices you make ultimately either improve the lives of the people around you or they hold them back. So, if you *feel good*, you are more likely to *do good*– both for yourself and for others. Those who flat out deny the power of material things to make us feel a certain way, positive or negative, are not being totally honest with themselves.

Picture yourself driving around in your dream car. How does it feel? Do you feel like somebody who is driving around a Nissan Maxima and can't pay your bills? Or do you feel like somebody who is ready to provide value to the world?

Now, I'm not saying if you drive a Nissan Maxima there's something wrong with that. I drove one for five years. This is just an example. You might not care about cars at all. You might even feel happier in a Nissan Maxima than a Tesla Roadster, but the point I want to drive home is things you buy that increase your happiness to some degree are worthwhile indirect investments.

They can contribute to your peak mindset. Of course, you can't rely on them fully. Material items are fun for a while, and then they become your new normal. But that's a good thing because if you expect to have the best, then you must also expect the best out of yourself.

When you're on the phone doing a business deal that has the potential to change the lives of thousands of people, your future customers or clients, do you want to go into that conversation expecting the best possible outcome? Or an average outcome? Going back to the car example, do you want to feel like the person driving the Bugatti? Or the Camry?

You don't buy nice things to impress other people. You buy them so your external state can match your internal state. And, by the way, this doesn't work the opposite way. You can't buy "cool stuff" and expect it to change you. But if you've worked hard on yourself internally, external things can help anchor your internal state in a positive place.

Another great example is your house. I love my house here in Florida. When I wake up here in the mornings, I feel great. I walk around, and I enjoy the high ceilings and the view I have of the golf course and my pool in the backyard. My home feels good to me, and I feel good here physically. This translates into my overall mindset.

When I wake up at home, I'm instantly filled with gratitude for my life and the blessings I have. Then, when I go out into the world, I feel like I'm living with a higher level of energy. This allows me to see more opportunity and leave better impressions on people. These two abilities are key in business.

If you can see opportunity and leave good impressions on people, that's all you need to succeed in business. These abilities are soft skills that are impacted directly by how good you actually feel. The hard skills for whatever you might need to get done—you can learn those, especially if you feel good about yourself and your ability to do so.

I'm not saying you need to go out and spend a bunch of money on toys to make yourself feel confident. But you should be making indirect investments in yourself from day one as an entrepreneur. If you just closed your first big deal, you should celebrate! Go out to a nice restaurant you normally wouldn't go to, and buy yourself a nice meal. Buy yourself something you want, just to show yourself some appreciation. An indirect investment doesn't have to be an expensive thing. It could just be a latte some morning if that is special for you, but it has to be something that makes you, *personally*, feel good.

In the end, everything is about the meaning you give it. You might be wondering why the big example I gave you to start was buying a nice car. The reason is because, for me, the meaning I attached to being able to own a Lamborghini at a young age has driven me to expect more out of myself since high school.

At sixteen years old, I was in Florida visiting my grandma, and a friend and I took my grandma's minivan out to get dinner. We pulled up at the restaurant right next to this guy who looked like he was under thirty, and he was sitting there in the parking lot in a gorgeous Lamborghini. I immediately thought to myself, "What the hell? How does that guy have a Lamborghini? He looks so young, and that's so much money!"

At the time, I was making less than $12 an hour working at an ice-cream shop, and I needed to know how the young guy sitting in the Lamborghini next to us had gotten to where he was in life so quickly. So, I did what any star struck sixteen-year-old would do. I rolled down the window and yelled at him, "Hey, man!" He looked over at me and my friend sitting my grandma's minivan, and I asked him with wide eyes, "What do you do?"

"I trade commodities," he said. Then he revved the engine and pulled away, probably laughing.

At sixteen years old, I had no clue what "I trade commodities" meant. But I turned to my friend and said very enthusiastically, "We've got to trade commodities!"

To me, that dude sitting in the Lamborghini next to me and my friend that day was the epitome of cool. And the car he was driving became a symbol of success and achievement for me from that day forward. It became a goal of mine to drive a Lamborghini before the age of twenty-five. I finally got one at age twenty-six.

I fully recognize not everybody wants the same things in life. You may want to live by the water somewhere tropical and not even own a car. You may want to have your own little hut in the woods where you can go and be by yourself whenever you want. Whatever it is you want, when you attain those things, it will boost your confidence because you will have gone through all the struggle required to get them, and you will have stayed true to yourself.

Yes, it is possible to get distracted by stuff. If you only want a certain thing because of the way you think it will make people view you, that's not something worth going after. But if you want something for yourself because you know it will bring you enjoyment, go after it!

We all have different goals and desires. Sometimes we can reach our goals and take hold of what we desire faster than we think is possible. For example, I set a goal for myself when I started drop-shipping. I wanted to do an additional $250,000 in revenue by the end of year one. I proceeded to blow past this goal in five days. Immediately, I was ready to get to work on my next goal.

As an entrepreneur, you have to be dedicated to growth more than anything else. If you are only dedicated to acquiring material things, chances are you will get them. But just beyond that experience will come complacency and disappointment. This is why you have to acknowledge the role indirect investments can play in your life early on in your journey as an entrepreneur, but you can't live for them. You must live and work for growth.

I have been fortunate to experience rapid growth in all of my businesses that have seen any sort of success. Of course, many of my attempts in business have gone nowhere, but the ones that have seen small success I've been able to scale up and grow quickly.

I absolutely love growing businesses. I love setting goals, crushing them, and then turning around and starting work on another one. But on a deeper level, even goal setting and business growing are external things that simply push us forward in life. I believe all of life is about mastering yourself. Happiness can't come from anything external or material. Material things can aid you in winning, but they can't make you fall in love with the game.

The real excitement and pleasure you get out of accomplishing things in life is found in figuring out more about who you are as you make progress. When you face new challenges at higher levels, this always forces you to dig deeper for the gold within yourself.

I love business because it allows me to consistently learn about myself. I consistently look at the things I thought I knew two years ago about business and life, and I say to myself, "Wow, things are actually much different than I thought."

According to Buddhist philosophy, it's possible to reach a point in life called enlightenment where you experience peak happiness and transcend past the problems of the material world. I don't know if this is possible, because I can't say I'm there yet, but it is certainly a worthwhile ideal to strive for in my opinion.

To me, enlightenment is the place you reach when you know you've done all you can to live the best life possible. However, I'm not sure if we can experience this until our lives come to a close. Until then, there is always more to discover about ourselves, and there is always more joy to be found in the present moment. There is no end to the mastery of self and the mastery of awareness.

Awareness is what brings us joy as living human beings. And practicing greater awareness is something we can always do, whether we're surrounded by the best things money can buy, or if we have none of the material things we desire at the moment.

Our sense of presence in our own lives can always increase. Treating ourselves well and going after what we want in life, material or otherwise, is natural and good for our personal development as long as we are true to ourselves. As entrepreneurs, we have the opportunity to change the world in a profound way. But, remember, to change the world, we have to start by changing ourselves. That's not easy, but it is worth it.

Chapter 3

Your Journey is
Your Destination

Here's something most people will not tell you. There's no such thing as "making it." One day you will get to that imaginary place you believe you have to get to in order to "make it," only to realize you are further away than you ever thought possible.

This is because who you are and what you want are always evolving. As you grow and develop throughout life, your needs and desires change. This is a normal and healthy part of living a life focused on reaching your highest potential.

If you had asked me what I wanted out of life when I was eighteen years old, and you had showed me a glimpse of what my life is like right now at age twenty-eight, I would have said, "Oh my God, I figured it out. I made it!"

But now that I'm here, and now that I've done a lot of the incredible things I've always wanted to do, I've realized I am further away from "making it" right now than I have ever been.

Growth is the most basic component of life. If you're not growing as a person from day to day, month to month, and year to year, you're dying. Many people refuse to get out of their comfort zones their whole lives, and then they look back and realize they wasted their potential. But there is a better way to live.

Instead of playing it safe, you can push your limits. It's hard to do this at first, but it's the only way to discover who you are and what you want. By pushing your limits, you begin to see more opportunity in the world around you.

Picture yourself climbing all the way to the top of a mountain peak. You push yourself to get there. You finally make it, and you're out of breath.

Then, as you're standing there, where you believe to be the top of the mountain, recovering and taking in the view, you notice a narrow, rocky ledge that leads to an even higher vantage point, which you can only guess will provide an even better view of the vast landscape before you.

"There is no way I'm going to come this far and not make it all the way to the top," you say to yourself, so you start to move towards the ledge. As you begin to inch along it carefully, at first, you are terrified, but soon it's over. Now you're really at the top, and the view is even more beautiful than you expected! You are so glad you faced your fears and climbed higher. Now you're ready to begin your descent down the mountain.

But before you go down, you decide to do a complete 360-degree turn to take in the full view, and just as you've almost turned all the way around, you notice another ledge leading up even higher!

This is a perfect illustration of what happens when you achieve something incredible in life you never thought possible. As you keep raising the bar on what you believe is possible, you begin to see things on a much bigger, grander scale. There is always higher to climb because the whole world begins to open up as you continue to develop a greater vision of what's possible.

Billionaire Naveen Jain, who is currently developing recreational space travel to the moon, said this about the importance of having a grand vision as an entrepreneur: "When I tell people what I'm working on, the first thing they tell me is that I'm crazy. And, to me, this is a sure sign that you are doing something meaningful. For someone to tell you, 'You are crazy,' that's when you are thinking big! And that's what moves the world forward."

Everything you do and create in your life expands your mind. Expansive awareness and the ability to dream big is not *normal*. Sadly, it's an ability most people have lost by the time they reach high school. But if you allow yourself to believe in the possibilities, there is always more to do. There are always bigger dreams to dream. That's what makes life so exciting and enjoyable!

Even though I have my dream life right now, I haven't accomplished anywhere near what I want to accomplish before my time is up. In fact, I don't expect to ever stop going after more.

On one hand, I am satisfied and thankful for all I have and all I have done. But I know my job is to keep pushing forward, even though I could stop right now, never work on another project, and live my life comfortably from here on out.

I am conscious of the fact there is no end destination, just the illusion of the highest goal my mind has conceived of at this moment. But once I am there, I know even my biggest goals will be replaced by bigger ones I could not have thought of in the past.

There is no possible way to get to the imaginary "there." Believing it is possible to ever "arrive" is dangerous because searching for a concrete destination in life means searching for disappointment.

So, if there is nowhere to get to, what should be the driving force behind our actions and goals? The answer lies in learning to enjoy the journey. I don't care how many times you've heard this phrase; until you let it sink in and realize just how true it is, you will always be disappointed with your life.

Life itself is a journey. It is meant to be experienced. If you can find a way to let go of the feelings of struggle we all experience as human beings, true happiness can be found.

What if you could be one hundred percent satisfied with your life right now, as it is? It might feel impossible, and you might not even want to try to feel happy if you're going through a very bad situation right now. But what if I told you the secret to getting more good things in your life was to appreciate the good things you already have? Would that change your whole approach to life?

The desire you have for more is not bad. It's just a sign you're still alive
and still on your journey. No matter how satisfied you become, you will still want more. But you absolutely have to balance this desire for more with appreciation for what you already have. If you don't consciously practice this balance, you can have everything and still feel like you're broke.

The truth is, when you get to age sixty, you're still going to want more. I'm not talking about more in terms of just material items. 'More' at age sixty might mean a deeper love for your family, a better spiritual connection with yourself, or a greater ability to pass on all of the wisdom you've acquired over the years to the next generation.

The desire to have more, be more, and do more in life never dries up. Being willing to acknowledge this changes everything. The ability to see the big picture, even when you're engrossed in the details, is the key to keeping your head above water when life is hard, and it's also the key to keeping yourself marching forward towards even more progress when life is going great.

The present moment is the only thing we have. The past, we forget, even if we try our best not to. The future, we can never predict. The present moment contains everything that is real, and it's the only place where we can either choose to be happy and grateful or miserable and unappreciative.

Every single one of us has something we can be grateful for. Even if you live in a crappy apartment with loud neighbors you don't like, even if your car barely starts every morning, even if you don't have the relationship you dream about in your life right now, there is something small you can be grateful for. Start there.

Maybe it's the ability to go out into nature and take in the beauty of the world around you. Maybe it's the ability to travel and not be tied down by different obligations. Maybe it's the ability to be alone in a safe environment and just focus on developing yourself mentally or spiritually. Through gratitude, your sense of personal power and responsibility are able to grow.

Having an intense focus on self-development is absolutely essential, especially if you want to be a successful entrepreneur. Self-development means taking responsibility for every area of your life first, before you go out and try to help anybody else.

You can see why this focus is necessary for an entrepreneur. An entrepreneur's success in business is determined by how well he can solve problems for other people. Solving problems is what generates value, and value is what generates money. But an entrepreneur can't do anything for anyone else for a long period of time unless he is continually developing himself.

Sometimes people ask me what keeps me motivated to keep moving towards my goals in life and business. I always encourage people to dream big, but the problem is when somebody tries to do this for the first time in their life, it's hard. They start to focus on how far they have to go, and the idea of all the stuff they're going to have to do to get to the end goal becomes overwhelming.

You and I already know the ultimate answer to this problem: there is no end. There is no having "made it." But since we know that, what should we do after we've set our sights on greatness?

First, let go of the need to get there. It's important to know where you want to go, but too much thinking about it can make you want to give up if you haven't yet had any kind of success. Second, focus only on doing the small things you know will help you make progress towards your big goal. The *how* and *when* of your big goal will take care of themselves.

If you think about success and goal achievement this way, it becomes easy. The problem is most people don't trust this process, and they don't trust themselves. They think success is all about luck, who you know, and what you know. But success is simple cause and effect. Do what you know you should do right now, and the effect of doing so will be success in the future.

If you want to know the secret to how I've created success for myself, and the secret other successful people have used to create success for themselves, it's *not* that myself or anyone else who is successful is more motivated than anybody else.

We all get motivated to achieve here and there. But great work is never accomplished based off of motivation alone. You can't wait until you feel motivated to work if you want to do anything worthwhile. Because, in most cases, anything that's worthwhile is going to be hard and painful to work on.

That's why the secret to success is not motivation, but discipline. I know this does not sound exciting, but I'm going to explain to you why it's vitally important for you to develop discipline if you want to make serious progress in your life and business.

For all of us, even those at the highest levels in any area of life, in the best-case scenario, we might wake up in the morning feeling motivated once or twice a week. However, it is totally normal, even for high-achieving people, to not feel motivated to do anything for two to three weeks at a time, especially if they have huge goals.

Notice I said high-achieving people don't *feel motivated* to do anything sometimes. That doesn't mean they follow that feeling and do nothing. It also doesn't mean they don't do everything they possibly can to induce a peak mindset in themselves every single day.

People who succeed at a high level are disciplined when it comes to taking the actions they know they need to take in order to induce a state in themselves beyond mere human motivation. When they are disciplined in taking these actions, the result is they tap into a layer of the human psyche that makes them say to themselves, "There is no possible way I'm not getting my work done today! This is nonnegotiable."

Here are some examples of things I have disciplined myself to do in order to induce a peak mindset. Your task is to experiment with the ideas I'm going to give you and the ideas you have heard other successful people talk about until you find what works the best for you.

In order to induce a peak state of awareness, I have to wake up early every morning. This requires major discipline because every night when I go to bed, I know I have to get up when my alarm goes off. But when it goes off in the morning, my brain always says to me, "No, Jared, you should rest more. You should lie back down. It'll feel good."

When I reply, "No, I'm getting up," I have just taken my first disciplined action of the day, and I'm now one step closer to inducing a peak mindset beyond human motivation.

Remember, discipline is what leads to success. My mind and my feelings, which most people rely on to guide their actions and motivation, do not want to get up out of bed. But

29

the better part of me, the part that knows what needs done, pushes me out of bed and one step closer to my goals.

If you rely on the feeling of motivation to get you out of bed in the morning, you're never going to do it. If you can't even make yourself feel "motivated" to get out of bed in the morning, how are you going to get yourself to do the work required to create your own successful business?

If you don't have motivation all the time, congratulations! You're human. If you've tried to make yourself more motivated and failed a thousand times, congratulations again! You've taught yourself a valuable lesson, even if you haven't realized it yet. That lesson is *you can't develop motivation*. But you can develop discipline, and discipline is what will get you results and put you in the peak mindset necessary for you to succeed.

There are two categories of discipline to take into account. The first category of discipline deals with the macro view. The macro view is the big picture. This is the discipline of setting large long-term goals and then periodically coming back to check on how you are progressing towards them. This is essential, and you can't lose sight of it, even though most of your time is going to be spent working in the second category of discipline.

The second category of discipline deals with the micro view. These are the hourly, daily, weekly, and monthly things you need to do to keep yourself on track towards accomplishing your large goals. Here is how I stay disciplined in this category.

Every Sunday, I take about two hours to look through all my notes and to-do lists from the previous Sunday, and I plan out what things I need to attack in the coming week. Everything I need to do, whether it's a big thing or a little thing, I write down.

Once I've done this, I then put all my time obligations down on my calendar for the week. This catches everything from meetings I need to have with my team, to what time I'm going to eat breakfast and go to the gym.

For every Monday, Tuesday, Wednesday, Thursday, and Friday, I also plan what time I'm going to wake up, what time I'm going to do my morning routine, and what time I'm going to start working.

Once I've done this, I then plan my work blocks. For work blocks, I don't say what work I'm going to do during a specific time as I'm planning the blocks at first. I just specifically reserve the time for work tasks on my calendar. I use this time to work on creative projects in an undistracted way.

After I've planned out my hours and days, I then go through my to-do list and figure out what I should allocate my time to within the work blocks I have available. I look at everything I need to get done, prioritize it, and schedule it.

Doing all of this preparation requires discipline, but it also creates discipline on another layer. With everything planned out for my week, I can know at a glance exactly what I am supposed to be doing at every moment of the day. If I'm not doing what was planned, then there should be a good reason for that. If there is an emergency, or if some unforeseen positive opportunity comes up, that might be a reason to deviate from the schedule.

Even then, I need to know when I have deviated from the plan. Having an action plan I can follow every single week allows me to monitor and measure the actions I'm taking and whether or not they're setting me up to hit the target.

Without this micro view of everything that needs to be done from hour to hour, day to day, and week to week, how disciplined you are being in your actions is almost impossible to quantify, especially over the long-term.

You might think you're being very disciplined because you have been working on something hard you don't want to do for a day, a week, or even a month, but unless you keep going no matter what, you may quit before you ever experience the result you're looking for.

Human beings do not understand how much time or effort we have actually put into something over time unless we measure it carefully. Our feelings are terrible at telling us reliably if we should speed up, slow down, or stop completely when it comes to any kind of long-term project. This is why, unless you measure your action and progress at the micro level, you will not hit your target.

There are two different "yous" constantly at war with each other whenever you are trying to do something good and accomplish something significant. If you don't believe me, let's look at a human phenomenon everyone has experienced—you in the morning is not the same person as you at night.

Have you ever laid in bed at night with your thoughts racing and your mind full of great ideas? Have you ever solved every problem in your life while lying wide awake in bed at 2:00 a.m., only to wake up the next day and come to the conclusion that all the solutions you came up with in the middle of the night are absolutely worthless?

That's proof you have two opposing forces within you— the creator and the critic. Which one is telling you the truth is up to you to decide. It's okay to doubt your ideas sometimes. That's normal, and sometimes it forces you to come up with better ones.

But the only true test of an idea is to come up with an action plan to test it with and then execute on it every single day. If you don't have a micro-level action plan you can take disciplined action on every morning when you wake up, you can forget about accomplishing any big goal you have over the long-term.

Without an action plan, you might wake up some mornings and be able to figure out the next step you should take. But the other you, the critic, is going to fight back. The other you is going to say, "Are you sure about that? That doesn't seem right. Let's just relax until we feel motivated; then we'll do something that's for sure right and productive." This is what makes "figuring out what you need to do today," every single day, an impossible task.

When I don't know exactly what I need to do, I feel scattered, and I take scattered, random action. This is what plagues almost every beginner entrepreneur. Without a top-down plan, most beginner entrepreneurs are lost, and they don't even know they need to come up with an action plan. So they do random things, and they hope for the best. This does not work, and it isn't sustainable.

As my business has grown over the last few years, I've naturally taken on more and more responsibilities. This means I don't have time to do any guesswork. If I waste the time I have available, it becomes impossible for me to get anything meaningful done. I don't want to spend every day doing maintenance tasks that only keep my business where it's at. I want to always be moving forward.

Now, you may not think all this discipline stuff matters a whole lot to you at this point. Maybe your business is not that big yet, or maybe your life isn't all that complex, so your business is the only thing you've got on your plate. Maybe right now you can float all of your to-do lists in your mind, and the thought of writing down everything you're going to do just sounds like busywork.

If you're managing everything just fine without doing any planning, why start this practice of planning everything you do and sticking to the plan? The reason you have to do this is because unless you are disciplined and plan your hours, days, and weeks, your business will not grow. Learning how to plan is a foundational skill all entrepreneurs must learn at some point.

It is better to build this foundation in the beginning, when you can still afford to screw it up as many times as possible while figuring out the best system for you. If you try to learn this skill when your to-do lists are a mile long, and your responsibilities are beginning to become more complex, it's too late.

Entrepreneurs don't have other people telling them what to do every day. This is one of the most compelling reasons people pursue entrepreneurship in general, but most beginner entrepreneurs are surprised to find the pressure does not let up just because you're the boss.

Instead, it just changes into a different form because your sense of personal responsibility must be extremely high at all times as a business owner. If it's not, your business will not survive.

As my businesses have grown, I've had to become obsessive about mastering my time to an extreme level. This means I'm constantly dealing with discomfort, and I'm constantly challenging myself to do new things, even when I don't want to.

What I've learned is every aspect of life and business is interconnected. So, if you can find a way to develop positive traits that will help you in business and in life through some form of daily practice, over time you will gain an extreme advantage.

For example, I practice taking cold showers every day. This trains my mind to take action when confronted with fear and discomfort. Learning how to break through fear is one of the most important things you can do because on the other side of fear is usually a reward. If not a reward, at least peace of mind.

Successful entrepreneurs must be masters of fear because every day presents new and often unpleasant challenges. Whether you need to let go of an employee, have an uncomfortable phone call with a manufacturer, or look at some numbers for the quarter you know aren't going to be good, you absolutely cannot run away from this stuff, even if fear is telling you that you should. You must push through the fear, and embrace the discomfort.

But you don't have to wait for an opportunity to embrace fear and discomfort to present itself in your business or in your life. You can start practicing embracing fear and discomfort by taking cold showers.

I can't tell you how many cold showers I've taken, and still, to this day, even though I know it's not going to hurt me whatsoever, when I turn on that cold water, something in my mind says, "Don't get in there. You're going to freeze to death."

Oddly enough, that's exactly what I want my mind to say. Because as soon as my mind says that, I jump in. I don't let that thinking hold me back. When I do this in the morning, it sets the tone for my whole day.

I know, intellectually, a cold shower is good for me. It boosts the immune system, improves circulation, and has many other health benefits. Even though I know it does all this for my body, that's not enough to make my mind quiet down when I'm about to jump into the cold water.

But as I've consistently practiced this over and over, I've noticed I don't take the fearful thoughts about getting into the water as seriously anymore. So, when fearful thoughts break into my mind when I'm looking at a situation that's new or challenging in life or business, I can apply the same mental strength I've developed through taking cold showers to the situation and break through to the other side of it quickly.

The best way to drive away a situation that's causing you fear in life is to jump in and take care of it right away. Most of the time, problems that seem big at first turn out to be small when you are proactive about them. But if you're not proactive, and you let fear grow, then problems grow too.

Let me give you an example from my life. Not too long ago, I had to let go of one of my team's first sales reps. I knew doing this was what was best for the company, and ultimately best for the rep, too, but I still didn't want to do it. I let it eat at me for almost two weeks.

I kept running the situation through my head and thinking, "What's the best way to do it? Should I take him out to lunch, try to have a good conversation, and end things on good terms?"

No idea I came up with in my mind for how to break the news to the guy made me feel better about having to do it. So instead of just getting it over with, I psyched myself out about it.

Then, one weekend while I was driving somewhere, I thought to myself, "I need to do it this week." I still wasn't being completely honest with myself, because I knew that, really, I needed to have done it already, but it was a Sunday. And I didn't want to call on a Sunday.

Finally, I became aware of what was really going on—I was letting fear keep me from doing what I knew needed to be done right that instant. So I said to myself, "You know what, Jared? You're always telling people to jump in and do the things they know they're supposed to do, even if they're fearful of them. Now it's time to practice that yourself."

Once I realized that, there was no letting myself off the hook for another day or another hour. Not even another minute. I took out my phone, called the guy, and proceeded to deliver the news to him in the most straightforward and honest way I could. And you know what? It was not that bad. It was uncomfortable, but I got it done, and then I didn't have to continue thinking about it and dreading it all week long.

When you start thinking about something you have to do that you don't want to do, over and over and over, it just becomes more stressful. You start to build a huge, intimidating picture of the task before you that's not even true to reality.

On top of that, the time you waste thinking about how much you don't want to do a particular thing allows other stuff you should be taking care of right now to pile up. This is how

36

people end up with an endless backlog of tasks on their to-do lists, and that's when the pressure really cranks up.

This is why discipline is so important. Though it sounds difficult, you have to understand, everything you do out of discipline reduces the amount of pressure and stress you're going to experience in the future. Doing the right thing today, that you don't want to do, puts you in the right position tomorrow to do all the things you would love to do.

Discipline is the most important part of attaining self and of attaining mastery in whatever you've decided to focus on in your life. To make discipline a habit, you have to fall in love with it. That's hard at first, because the results of being disciplined aren't always obvious. But discipline is the only thing that produces results. And once you have results—well, results are easy to fall in love with.

Part of attaining self is attaining happiness and contentment with whatever you have in the present moment. That's why meditation is another practice I have found to be extremely important for inducing a peak mindset.

It's difficult to sit in silence for twenty minutes and just allow feelings and thoughts to come and go. Sometimes the twenty minutes fly by, and other times, after eight minutes, the last thing you want to do is sit there for another twelve.

When time is passing slowly and painfully in meditation, it's very tempting to say, "Okay, I meditated for eight minutes. That's good enough," and then get up and go about your day. But if you constantly don't follow through in sticking to the time you've allotted for meditation, you are yet again setting a precedent for how you will act when anything in your life or business isn't progressing as fast as you think it should be.

Meditation, as I practice it in my daily life, is the continuous training of present-moment awareness. Meditation isn't something you can do once and then expect to benefit from. Doing meditation continuously, even when it doesn't feel good, is how you produce all the benefits of meditation in your life.

When you sit down day after day to meditate, no matter what, eventually the anxiousness about when the ending timer is going to go off disappears. Even better than that, the feeling I described at the beginning of this chapter that causes us to constantly ask ourselves, "When am I going to *arrive*? When am I going to *make it*?" – that also disappears.

When you start to see the benefits of living from the state of present-moment awareness and flow that can be accessed through meditation, then everything in your life gets better. It gets better because when you live in the present moment, you become aware enough to realize how all of your actions in every moment influence your results.

Once you are aware of that, you can trace your results back to their source. And when you do this, what you will find is all positive results are derived from discipline and focused action. When you come to know this for yourself, then comes the best part. You are able to fall in love with discipline and focused action because you recognize that these things, though they may seem unpleasant, are the only things that allow you to become a better person.

With this understanding, every morning you wake up feeling groggy, tired, and unmotivated, you now know you have the power to turn it around. You have the power to induce a peak mindset through discipline and focused action and create the best day of your life, every single day.

Now, you might be thinking, "Okay, I understand all of this, but I don't know if I believe it. To me, forcing myself to be disciplined sounds more like prison than the path to success."

But let me ask you this. Do you want to continue getting the results you've been getting in your business and in your life? Do you want to continue to live with your current limitations, be they financial or otherwise?

My guess is you don't, or you wouldn't have picked up this book. So here's what you need to realize. Your comfort zone and/or lack of discipline is the true prison. When you master discipline, you master yourself. And when you master yourself, you attain self. When you attain self, there is no goal or dream too big for you to accomplish.

You can read this entire book. You can learn all you want from other people about what you should and shouldn't do to live a good life and be successful in business, but you will never truly understand what's important for you to know and to do until you start practicing discipline and learn to fall in love with it.

Once you commit to the process of attaining self through this route, you will come to the realization, as I have, that there is no "there." You can never "make it." Your journey is your destination, so enjoy every moment.

Chapter 4

Focus on the Person You Need to Become

This is how most people live. They do the bare minimum required to check all the boxes, and then they wonder why they don't feel happy and fulfilled. It doesn't even occur to them they should be reaching for more, not just in terms of what they can accomplish, but in terms of who they are as a human being.

It's very important to create a mental picture of who you want to be in the future. For example, if you're in your twenties, who you want to be in your thirties might be totally different than who you want to be when you're twenty-five. Additionally, who you want to be when you're forty might look totally different than who you want to be when you're thirty-five, etc.

It's okay to go with the flow and find your way through life as you go, but it's important to have a visual picture in the back of your mind of what you want your life to look like in the future. If you want to be a passionate leader, and you want people to respect you and appreciate your contributions to the world, then you have to know what that passionate, respected, and contributive leader is going to look like. This is the best version of yourself you can imagine.

Who you are right now is not capable of doing the great things you intend to do in the future. If you were, you would have already done them or be doing them. Your focus must be on personal development so you can become the person who perfectly aligns with your future goals. Then, when the actions you need to take present themselves, you will be able to complete them and reach your goals with certainty.

In my experience, if you aren't presently living in a state of happiness, gratitude, certainty, and personal power, you can't just "think" your way into feeling more happy, grateful, certain, or powerful. You have to begin to develop your mental capacity to feel these things through a different route.

The secret is it doesn't start with your mind. You can't just lie in your bed or on your couch all day and think about how great you are. That's not going to work. You have to get up and do something. You have to move your body, get your blood flowing, and increase your capacity for feeling a greater sense of vitality and awareness.

There are different things you can do to get your body moving. You don't have to be an Olympic athlete to take advantage of the benefits of exercise in your life. Getting up and going for a walk outside early in the morning, or doing stretches in your living room before you start your day can make a huge difference in your overall experience of life.

Focusing on your body and yourself like this is so important. The lie we've been told is that it's wrong to focus on ourselves. We've been told it's selfish to want the best for ourselves, or that if we spend too much time thinking about how we can improve our lives, we're going to forget about everybody else around us who needs our attention.

But unless we take care of ourselves first, we're not going to be of use to anybody else. If you spend all your time putting out other people's fires, eventually you're going to run out of water. Then what are you going to do when your own house goes up in flames?

You need to learn how to balance your body and mind to become the best version of yourself possible. If you're depressed and feeling down, there's sometimes nothing you can think in your brain to make yourself feel better. Then the depression starts to take over your physical body, and you become sedentary.

So, to get to the mind and change that, you have to get out and move when you're not feeling good. If you're not feeling one hundred percent, which is normal, just start moving. Go to the gym. Lift weights. Run. Do yoga or stretch. Start somewhere with your physical body, and do whatever you can do. To become the best version of yourself, you have to develop a better state of mind by increasing your physical awareness and fitness level.

Pound your chest. Jump up and down. Do some breathing exercises. Because when your body gets moving, you'll start to feel better, and you'll create more energy that can flow through you. This will increase your ability to focus and allow you to generate a clearer vision of your future.

When your body feels good, you can literally see more opportunity in the world around you. Then, when you successfully take action on the opportunity you see around you, your mind grows stronger. When your mind grows strong and confident, then you can effortlessly attract more good things into your life.

The key takeaway here is your overall well-being begins with your body. Most of us think we can just sit in one place and convince ourselves to feel happy, but that's almost impossible. We have to focus on the physical first. Even a simple change such as improving your posture actually sends a signal to your brain that will make you more confident.

If you stand tall and stand strong, you will feel strong and powerful mentally. And it's a lot more fun to live life with a sense of strength and power than it is live in fear about what could happen next. If you hold fear in your mind, your body language and your energy will repel people away from you. But if you hold confidence in your mind, your presence will give off a powerful, attractive quality to others.

Your presence, communication ability, and energy all start in your physical body. Most people have forgotten this because, in the modern world, our physical body is typically the last thing we think about over the course of the day if we think about it at all. It's so easy to live in a world made entirely of emails, texts, social media, phone calls, and video chats. A modern-day entrepreneur can theoretically run a million-dollar business while never getting out of bed.

The only problem is, we're not just mental creatures. The body plays an integral role in our emotions and ability to think, and unless we use it regularly, there's no way we'll have the energy necessary to run a successful business.

If you start your day by checking your phone for texts, calls, and emails, and then you immediately start responding to a bunch of people, this will put you into a reactive, sedentary state. Do you think this state is nearly as effective as the state you would be in if you jumped out of bed in the morning, went for a run, took a cold shower, listened to some good music, got pumped up for the day, and then sent those same texts and emails and made those same calls?

Engaging your body and your mind first thing in the morning leads to exponentially more effective results. To get your first big win in business, or to keep winning consistently, you have to be at your best at all times.

This is because you never know when the effect of being at your best is going to click into place with the right moment and opportunity and produce the massive result you've been looking for. High energy means high potential. When you're going to need to release high energy, you can't predict. But your energy potential must be constantly developed in preparation for that time.

If your energy is low, the conversations you have with other people will not develop properly. This can lead you to miss out on opportunities that could change your entire life and the lives of others. There are infinite possibilities available to every single one of us in life. To give yourself the best chance to act on these possibilities, you have to be functioning at your best, both physically and mentally, 24/7/365.

A lot of people starting out in business don't realize this. We've been taught that if you want to succeed in business, you have to sacrifice. This is true, but it's important to specify what things should be sacrificed and what things absolutely cannot be sacrificed for any reason.

Most people sacrifice the wrong things and wonder why they're not getting anywhere with their business. They sacrifice their sleep, diet, personal relationships, and ultimately their health in order to get ahead, only to find themselves slowly falling behind.

They think to themselves, "I don't have time for that stuff! I need to work on my business. Once I have money, then I can think about my personal health." This is a losing strategy. If you choose to be reactive about your health, you are going to pay for it later on. And even if you somehow make a lot of money while not taking care of yourself, if you're not around to enjoy it, what's the point?

Your health is your first wealth. Be proactive about it. Build a good foundation to stand on. If you are reactive about taking care of anything in your life, whether that be your health, your relationships, or your spiritual connection, what's really happening is you're being pushed further and further out of your zone. A reactive approach to life, even if you are able to get by at an acceptable level, will always leave you out of balance.

When you are out of balance, you can't get into the zone with your business, your relationships, your family, or your spiritual life. Every good thing in life requires proactive development, and that's why most people spend their lives waiting for a lucky break that never comes. Or worse—they don't even believe their life can improve in any way, ever.

There is no doubt the responsibilities of life can be overwhelming, especially for beginner entrepreneurs. Most have full-time jobs, sometimes they have families to look after, and they also need time for themselves.

This is why starting a business is hard work, and most people quit before they succeed. They get caught in a routine of waking up in the morning just before they have to rush out the door. They eat a fast and unhealthy breakfast because they have no time to think about what they're putting into their body. Then they get to the office, and they sit all day at their desk. By the time it's time to come home, their energy is depleted, and they just want to relax.

Then they remember they want to escape this cycle, but they're too tired to try. They tell themselves, "I'll start tomorrow," but "tomorrow" never comes.

So, if you want to get out of this situation, here's what you should do first—prioritize your personal development. This is because, as Tony Robbins' mentor Jim Rohn wisely said, "Your level of success will seldom exceed your level of personal development because success is something you attract by the person you become."

If you are stuck in a reactive cycle of working for someone else, neglecting your body, and putting off your true ambitions, you have to find a way to carve out time to work on your own personal development first. Then, as you grow personally, your ability to carry out your business plans will naturally increase. From there, you can continue to work on yourself and your business until you have broken out of the cycle. However, your focus on developing yourself and your business can never stop, even after you've had success.

To give you an example of what this might look like, before I experienced sustainable success in business for myself, I worked for a social media app company full-time. I was fortunate because when I needed to be in the office was flexible. On most days, when I wasn't traveling, I went into the office at about 10:00 a.m.

This meant I could have stayed up late watching TV or partying every night, slept until 9:00 a.m., and still made it in to work on time. That's what a lot of people I worked with did. But since I knew I wanted to own my own business and not work for somebody else forever, I also could have chosen to go to work, put in my time, and then come home and give whatever energy I had left to working on myself and my business.

A lot of people's schedules force them to do it this way, and it's not a bad approach. But when I tried to do this, I quickly recognized the amount of energy I had available to use in a given day was limited. Energy and time are like money. If you have money, you don't want to invest it in things that don't produce anything of value for you.

The same thing goes for your time and energy. When you're working full-time and trying to start your own business, your time is extremely limited, so you don't want to spend it on anything that's not producing value for you and getting you where you want to go. The time you have available to work on yourself and your business, you can't increase, so you have to look at another variable, which is your energy.

There are certain ways you can increase your energy, which I have already discussed (getting your body moving, etc.), and there are also ways to maximize its potential.

Everyone who is just starting out as an entrepreneur has to consider how much energy and time they have available to dedicate to working on themselves and their goals.

Personally, I have always found my morning hours to be the most productive and energetic times of my day. So, when I was working full-time, I decided to get up every morning at 5:00 a.m. and hit the gym to increase my energy levels. Once I was done with my workout, this left me with three quality hours to work on my personal development and get things done for the hoverboard business I was working on at the time.

In addition to being able to increase my energy through exercise in the morning, I also enjoyed having peaceful and quiet time to myself before anything else could distract my attention for the day. This allowed me to remain in a proactive, opportunity-seeking state all day long.

If you want to start your own business while working full-time, here's the secret: *don't even worry about the business you're going to start.* Instead, start focusing on and preparing yourself for success, first and foremost. You do that by being as proactive as you can possibly be about every aspect of your life.

You don't have to be a reactive puppet in the world. You don't have to allow other people to pull your strings. Give yourself a chance to be proactive about doing what's best for you, whatever that may look like. Give yourself time to think and time to act.

Every human being needs time for themselves. It doesn't matter if you consider yourself an extrovert or an introvert. The majority of people don't take time to think for themselves these days because there is so much noise in our everyday environments.

There are many unhelpful, negative opinions out there that people are eager to share with us, not to mention the self-doubts and insecurities that always pop up when starting a business. A lot of people are scared to be alone with themselves because they've filled their minds with so much self-defeating information.

But spending time alone is the only way to figure out what you're going to do as an entrepreneur and who you want to be. Many people never take the time to figure out what direction they actually want to go in life. They are just rushed along by the education system, their parents, their friends, and their environment. It doesn't have to be this way.

Even if all you can do is set aside two hours in an entire week to spend time thinking, meditating, writing, coming up with ideas, creating action plans and implementing them, you will be well on your way to a better future. If you don't currently have two hours of free time per week, it's time to take a look at your priorities and start sacrificing the things you are doing that are producing nothing of value in your life.

For most people, that's social media time, Netflix, or going out with friends. The average person spends four hours per day just looking at their phone. And if you were to ask most people what they're looking for when they get on their phone, they don't even know. It's just a habit to look at it whenever they've got a free moment.

Now, you can live a comfortable life, go to work every day, and then come home and do whatever you want with your time. But living this way isn't going to produce anything extraordinary in your life. It's only going to produce what's normal, and what's normal is a person who is broke, unhappy, and bored.

If you want something different, and you want to succeed at a higher level, then you have to decide to be different. Do you want to have average results? Or do you want something better? If you want something better, you have to define what that looks like for you personally. That starts by taking the time to recognize where you're at right now and where you want to go.

Let's forget about the business side of things for a moment. Let's just say you haven't been looking after your health, and you're overweight and unhappy about it. Recognizing this is the reality is the first step. The second step is recognizing you need to make a change. The third step is deciding how much change needs to occur, and the fourth step is deciding how quickly it needs to occur.

Going through these four steps, you might decide you want to lose twenty pounds over the next six months. Once you've decided that, this is a clear goal you can take action towards achieving. Fortunately, the fifth step is very simple in today's world—finding a plan to follow. In this case, one that will help you lose the weight.

The worst excuse in the world right now when it comes to doing anything is saying you don't know what to do. We all have access to unlimited amounts of information on any topic at the click of a button. Sure, it can be overwhelming to choose between one plan of action or another, but in that case, look for someone who is clearly an expert at doing what you want to do, and see if they can help you in some way.

The resources you need to be successful in any area you choose are out there, but you still have to learn how to be resourceful. You also need to know yourself. What are you willing to do? What action plan will you execute to perfection?

It's on you to follow any plan, and this is the hardest part for people. It's also the reason why I told you focusing on self-development is the first step. You have to become the person who has enough self-integrity and grit to see a plan through before you can hope to succeed at a higher level than you currently are in any area of your life.

When you commit to following a plan to improve your life or start your own business, it can still take some time before what you're doing will start to feel natural. Any change in life is hard to make, even if it's a small one. You have to exercise discipline for just over two months before a new habit

49

becomes truly automatic, and it takes roughly twenty-one days to make a behavior habitual, depending on the person.

If you start to do something new and positive for three days, and then you slip up and do nothing for three days, that's not good. Not only did you derail your progress; you also hurt your self-integrity and confidence because you weren't true to yourself.

But when you are true to yourself, your self-confidence compounds over time. Every time you say you are going to do something, and you do it, you begin to take all of your commitments more seriously. You begin to believe in yourself with certainty, and build invaluable confidence.

And when you know, without a doubt, that you're a person who sticks to what they say they're going to do, no matter what, you become stronger and harder to break down. When nothing can make you quit, it's just a matter of time before you reach your goals. When you become the person you need to be to succeed, life will line you up with the right opportunities and take care of the rest. *I dare you to test this in your own life.*

Chapter 5

There is No Shortest
Route to Success

When you are looking forward and into the future, when you're trying to decide what series of events you'd like to happen, it's hard to make any sort of sense of life because there are so many different possibilities. Most of the time, what you expect to happen is not what actually happens.

When you're in the moment and experiencing something, especially something bad, it's very easy to ask yourself, "Why is this happening?" But when you get into the future, and you start to look at your past, then it all begins to make sense.

There is no doubt about it. Life is incredibly complex. One small action today could set off a chain reaction of things that will happen later in your life. For example, I could drop my phone right now, break it, and completely miss a call from somebody who wants to do a huge business deal with me. Because I didn't answer, they might decide to move on and make that deal with somebody else.

Knowing this can happen doesn't mean I live in fear of missing opportunities. It's just a great illustration of how many possibilities there really are, and how we will never be able to predict with certainty what type of success is going to stem from our next action. Since there are infinite possibilities in life, whatever small choices we make today, we have to make them knowing they have the potential to propel us into a vastly different future.

Anything can happen. There is no shortest route to success. In fact, you don't know the route to success, even if you think you do. I have achieved many of the things I have always dreamed of achieving in my own life, and I've taken note of the things I believe have led me to where I am today. But I still can't tell you exactly how your dreams are going to come true.

All I can do is give you principles to live by which I believe will help you, but your experience will be different than mine—in fact, you don't want to have my experience because you need to be true to yourself in order to experience fulfillment in life.

The advice you get from others, including me, can only move you further along on your own personal journey. That's it. You are going to experience objects blocking your path as you go along. There is no way to get around these hurdles because they are designed to prepare you for your future. *They aren't in the way.* When you take a look at the bigger picture, you will recognize *they are the way.*

The only thing you can do every single day is try to better your odds for success, and you do this by preparing yourself to become the best version possible of you. Even when something goes wrong, the truth is, it is likely pointing you in the right direction if you are willing to listen to your own intuition.

For example, as you know, with my concert promotion company, I lost all of my money on one big show. This was a huge pivotal moment in my life. It changed the direction of my future forever.

But it's not just huge pivotal moments that have the power to change the direction of your future. In fact, most of the time it's not the big, noticeable changes in direction that impact your life forever. Sometimes you don't even notice when serious change has occurred. The small daily choices you make are like a rudder on the ship of your life. When you turn this rudder ever so slightly, you end up somewhere completely different.

I've often thought to myself, "What if that arena show *had* worked? What if I'd succeeded with that one, and then kept on succeeding? What would my life look like if it was centered around throwing huge events, as the biggest concert promoter in the world?"

I don't know the answer to that question. My life could have been better than it is now, or it could have been worse. But from where I sit now, being an event promoter is the last thing I want to be doing. I love my businesses, and if I was still doing events, I wouldn't be where I am now, and this book would probably not be in your hands.

I fully believe in visualizing the best possible life you can imagine for yourself, which we'll talk more about in a later chapter. But to a certain extent, it's also important to let go. You don't know what success looks like for you. I certainly don't know what it looks like for you, and neither does anybody else.

The best thing you can do to put yourself in the best position to succeed is to follow your interests. For example, if you're interested in real estate, even if you don't know why that's the case, invest in real estate education for yourself.

Once you've educated yourself a little bit, go out there and do it. Fail, and fail some more. Do all you can in real estate until you want to give up, and even if you are forced to give up for some reason, that doesn't mean it's over for you. You can still find success. You might go back to real estate at some point with new wisdom about what you should try next, or you might find something else that suits you better.

Just getting started doing something increases your odds of success exponentially. Most people never even get started, and that's why they never end up getting to where they truly want to be.

Once you've found something you want to focus on and are interested in, start attending events related to it. Doing this will increase your odds of success. When you consciously put yourself in an environment with other people who are already doing what you want to do, this changes everything.

Instead of just learning by reading on your computer or by reading a book, which are still good things to do, when you're in an environment with people who are already successful, you are able to make valuable connections and get personal help breaking into the industry you've set your sights on.

Immersing yourself in the proper supportive environment will take you into a whole new level of reality, making what you want to do that much more possible. This is because there are different layers of belief that affect your likelihood of being able to achieve something. To gain the greatest possible chance of achieving something, you must do all you can do to enforce the belief that you can do it.

For example, let's say you want to climb Mount Everest, so you go online and look up a video on YouTube of somebody climbing Mount Everest. Watching this video affects your first layer of belief.

You see in this video that someone else out there has done the thing you want to do, in this case climbing Mount Everest, and this causes you to say to yourself, "Okay, I see that doing this is possible. Maybe it's possible I could do it, but probably not."

At this first layer of belief, you believe it's possible for someone to do what you want to do, but you don't yet transfer that possibility onto yourself. However, your interest is still captured, so you are willing to pursue it further.

So, you decide to rent and watch a documentary about a guy who climbed Mount Everest. You not only learn through this documentary that many people have climbed Mount Everest but also exactly how one particular person did it, step by step.

This experience affects your second layer of belief, so you say to yourself, "Okay, I see many people have done this, and now I actually know exactly how one person did it." You begin to believe you could do it if you did everything the person in the documentary did to prepare, but you are still not sure where to start, or if it's even worth it to put in all the work you now know, without a doubt, is going to be required.

A few weeks go by, and you can't stop thinking about climbing Mount Everest. So, you go online, and you stumble across somebody on social media who has actually climbed Mount Everest. You decide to send them a message about it, and they respond to you.

You get to ask all the questions you want about the experience and how the person specifically trained to climb the mountain. You are completely fascinated by what the person tells you, and you discover that when they were just getting started, they weren't sure they could do it either. But by following a certain training plan, they did it.

At this point, the reality of you actually climbing Mount Everest for yourself moves a little bit closer. You've talked with somebody who has done it. They've told you about the doubts they had in the beginning too, and that those are totally normal.

This affects your third layer of belief. You can almost picture yourself climbing Mount Everest now for yourself if you just had some help getting started and sticking to the intense training regimen.

Finally, noticing how interested you are in mountain climbing, the person you talked to online reaches out to you and invites you to a meet-up of about a hundred different people who all love to climb. You're not sure if you belong, since you've only ever climbed up your stairs, but you just can't let the opportunity pass you by.

So, you show up to the meet-up, and everyone there is practicing different exercises together. You meet some people who say they've been climbing their whole lives, and they tell you all the mountains they've submitted. These people want to help you out and give you all the tips and tricks they've learned. And there are even some beginners at the meet-up, learning new things right alongside you.

Now you've reached the fourth and deepest layer of belief. You are fully immersed in the complete picture of the reality that you *can* climb Mount Everest. You are ready to take action, and you do. You start training. You start working with everybody in the group. You are surprised to find that not only are they helping you, but you are helping them, too.

Then that fateful day comes. You ascend the mountain through sheer force of will, and now you stand at the top. Your dream has become a reality—all because you continued to pursue your interest. You brought the possibility closer and closer until you fully saturated all four layers of belief in yourself, making it more vivid and real to you with every step.

Now that you are on top of Mount Everest, you have a realization you did not expect to have. You realize, with absolute certainty, that you can climb not just Mount Everest, but any mountain you decide you want to climb.
You have now shattered the fifth and most important layer of belief I haven't even told you about yet. This is the layer you break through when you realize *you can do anything if you believe you can.*

I said earlier I cannot tell you the shortest route to success, and this is true. But I can give you the shortest route to the fifth layer of belief, which, in my opinion, is even more important. It's going to sound obvious when I say it: the shortest route to the fifth layer of belief, where you realize you can do anything if you believe you can, is to start at the fourth layer of belief. Meaning, surround yourself with people who are doing what you want to do.

The best way to do that as an entrepreneur is by going to live events such as Unleash the Power Within, 10X Con, Affiliate Summit, etc. Anywhere you can go and surround yourself with thousands of entrepreneurs who are all gathered together to work on their businesses and better themselves is a fantastic place to be if you want to shortcut right to your fourth layer of belief.

When you go to an event like this, it is a one hundred percent guarantee you will meet people in the flesh who are, right now, doing exactly what you want to be doing in the future. Not only do you give yourself the opportunity to expand your network and make meaningful connections that may serve you for the rest of your life, but you are also giving yourself the opportunity to provide value to other people who are looking for what you have to offer, even if you don't know what that is yet.

Contrast this experience with sitting at home on your computer all weekend reading about entrepreneurship. Don't get me wrong. There are a lot of worse things you could be doing with your time than that, but if you want to get to the good stuff as soon as possible in your business, do everything you can to start interacting with people who are already experiencing success. Most of the time, they will be willing to help you in some way. The quickest way to break through the fourth layer of belief to the fifth is to surround yourself with people operating from the fourth or fifth layer already.

Imagine you are bored at home one weekend, so you call your friend who is also sitting at home doing nothing. You guys decide to go to Applebee's. While you're there, you have a few drinks too many, gossip about the people from your hometown, and then go home to sleep. In the morning, you wake up with a hangover, and you realize it's going to take you half the day to nurse yourself back to a functional state.

If that sounds like your life right now, I want you to picture something better. What if, instead of doing that, you were proactive, and two weeks ago you decided that this weekend, you are going to go to a live event and surround yourself with people who are actively trying to improve their own lives?

Now it's Saturday morning, and you wake up excited for what you're about to experience. You drive to the event, and you don't know anybody. But you find your way to the first speaker, and immediately he gets you talking with the people around you, and you make some new friends. You find out, as fate would have it, your new friends are involved in a business that relates very well to the one you want to start.

What happens next? The possibilities are endless. The point is the net effect of surrounding yourself with these kinds of people is astronomically different than calling up your old buddy to go drink some beers at Applebee's.

I know going to a live event is not always possible every weekend. Due to budget or time constraints, it might not be possible for you at all right now. But going to a live event is not the only way you can start to surround yourself with people who can make a positive impact on your life.

It is commonly said we are the average of the five people we spend the most time with. Most people know this, but there's a question that often goes unanswered when people talk about this topic. How do you choose the right people to include in your life, and how much time should you actually spend with them?

First, you have to recognize there are three different groups of people in your life. This can be uncomfortable to come to terms with initially. I'm not saying you should treat any person in your life with any less respect because of what group you end up placing them in.

But you have to personally recognize some people are going to drag you down, some people are going to grow right alongside you, and others are far beyond where you're at in life, so they can help you make major leaps forward. The three groups of people I'm going to explain to you are important to understand, so you can decide how to allocate different percentages of your overall energy to each of them in your life.

Keep in mind; these groups are not static. As you grow and progress through life, where people fall within these groups is going to change. Your primary goal is to continue to surround yourself with people who are doing, have done, or want to do the things you want to do in the future. Let's jump right into it.

Group one people are the people you grew up with. These are typically your old friends from high school and college and other people you know that have just been doing the same old thing with their life for a while. You might have once connected with these people, but now your connection to them is not as strong.

You might have some old emotional connections to them that make you feel obligated to try to see them when you go home for the holidays and things like that, but, pretty much, nothing about your lives now or the lives each of you want is similar, making it hard for you to relate.

Group two people are your current peers. These are people who are operating at your current level. For example, if you're an internet marketer making $400,000 a year, these people are internet marketers making between $200,000 and $500,000 a year. Whatever you're doing, these people are on the exact same page as you.

Because of that, these people are able to hold you accountable. They understand your challenges, complement your weaknesses, and you can both be of value to each other on a daily basis. You look up to these people a little bit, but for the most part, you're on a level playing field. Your relationships with group two people are mutually beneficial. There's a healthy give and take involved.

Group three people are people you aspire to be like. These could be people who make a lot more money than you or people who are more physically, mentally, and spiritually evolved and advanced than you.

Group three people are people who live a lifestyle you adore. For example, a group three person could be a man who drives your dream car, has a happy family, and lives on the beach. If that's what you aspire for your life to be like, and you're not there yet, somebody who is doing those things would fall into your group three. Group three people are beyond where you are right now in your life in some way, shape, or form that matters to you.

Once you have identified where the people currently in your life fall within these three groups, the next step is to decide how you're going to allocate your energy among them. Here's how I suggest you do it if you want to experience the effects of maximum positive influence on your life.

When it comes to group one, you don't want to spend too much time with these people, or you will begin to lower your standards and subconscious beliefs down to their level. If you have a best friend from high school who means a lot to you, but happens to fall into this category, obviously you don't just cut them out of your life. But you still have to be careful how you allow them to influence you and the decisions you make.

A best friend like this is the only edge case in this group. They get grandfathered in. But when it comes to everybody else, you have to learn to let go of those old emotional

60

connections that no longer play a role in your life. It's time to cut the fat, and this means you don't have any obligation to spend time with group one people you don't have a real connection with.

There's one group of people I didn't put into any of the three groups—your family. I didn't put them into a group because everyone's family is different. For me, family means a lot. They get my attention when they need it, without question.

But other people don't necessarily have a great relationship with their family. Maybe their family is full of people who are a negative influence on them. In that case, you may not be able to completely cut ties with them, but you have to set clear boundaries for how you will and will not allow them to treat you. If you need space from your family in order to thrive in life, give it to yourself. You deserve it.

Let's move on to group two. Group two is perfect for you to be around all the time. When you spend all your time with this group, people in group one, maybe even that old best friend, will probably get mad.

But that's actually okay. You're not doing anything wrong. In the end, you may actually end up inspiring people in group one to raise their standards and level of personal responsibility. If they do that, they can be in your group two—just know you can't make anybody change their ways unless they decide to do so for themselves.

Group two people are the people you can count on. They're able to give you good advice, and they relate to you perfectly. You will naturally find yourself spending ninety percent of your time with group two people once you cut the fat in group one.

This gives you ten percent of your time left to spend with group three people. This works out well because even if you wanted to spend all your time with group three, that's not going to happen. People in group three got to the level they're at because they understand exactly what I'm talking about right now. I can guarantee you that.

Group three people do not go around looking for group two people to hang out with. They want to surround themselves with people already at their level. Sometimes it's possible to find a mentor who falls into group three, and in that case, you should treat your mentor with respect and do what they tell you to do. Because when it comes to group three people, the one thing they value the most is their time. If they're giving you their time, you shouldn't be wasting it by not following directions.

Now, here is the problem that plagues most beginner entrepreneurs—all they've got is group one people in their life. They don't know anybody who is actually trying to better themselves in any way, which would put them into group two. The average person does not even believe it's *possible* to change themselves or their current situation for the better.

So, if you're trying to change, which you are if you're reading this book, that puts you into your own group two, even if you haven't had any success yet. Until you have success, things might be a little bit lonely. But don't worry. The right people and circumstances will come into your life, little by little, when you make space for them by distancing yourself from group one and focusing on yourself.

You might feel bad about distancing yourself from group one people, but the truth is separation is going to happen anyway when you do have some success. There are two reasons for this.

Number one, once you have some success in changing your life, you won't be able to relate to the people who still believe that's not even possible. They're going to be meeting up at the bar to talk about how much they hate their boss, how they aren't making enough money, and how they can't afford their car payment. And you do not want to bring your energy down to that level by spending your time talking about those things.

Number two, when that's the kind of stuff people want to talk to you about, you can't just start a conversation with them about what you're doing and how great things are going for you. Even though these people may say they want success for you, when they see it happening for you, it's just going to make them mad, both at you and themselves. They will start thinking, "Ugh, why didn't I do that?"

If you're looking to group one people for support, you're not going to find it. They won't be able to celebrate your success with you because of their own envy, and if you face challenges, their only comment is going to be, "Yeah, that's why I didn't do that."

I don't know if you're ready to hear this or not, but at some point, you have to make a choice. Do you want to fit in with the people you've known all your life who are living below their potential or do you want to conquer your own life and rise to the top? If you want to conquer your life, get rid of the people in your life who you can't add value to and who can't add value to you.

What I've given you here are general rules to follow to help you allocate your time and energy. You may have to be more or less extreme with policing your time with these different groups based on your personal situation. You might be fortunate to have very positive and influential friends you've known since high school that you continue to keep in contact with today. In that case, you have to decide for yourself who in your life falls into what group.

But the important thing to remember here is that you absolutely must spend time grooming high-value relationships if you want to continue improving yourself. Finding group two and group three people to spend your time with takes time, and it's worth it to vet these people carefully before you allow them into your inner circle. Once you've found these people, you want to focus on providing as much value to them as you can.

Because, in the end, the more value you give others, the more value you receive. There's a great book on this topic I highly recommend called *The Go Giver*. I want to make it clear that you should never try to give value as a way of manipulating someone into helping you. That's just going to make you look fake.

You have to seriously internalize the importance of giving value for the sole reasons of a) it feels good, and b) it will improve your life and the lives of others in the future. In everything you do, be nice, and be sincere.

I don't consider myself a master networker. But if you're doing what you do best, and you're passionate about it, you don't have to be the most charming person in the world to make a strong impression on the right people.

You just need to realize the common principle of all good relationships is they involve a value exchange. If you add value to someone's life, and you're friendly in general, then you'll eventually get some time with people who are doing things beyond where you're at right now. From there, if you are sincere and friendly, you can turn that time into a friendship.

Be grateful for all the people in your life, even the negative influences. They can show you how not to be. Be grateful for the people who are in the same place as you right now. They can show you what you're doing right and support you through your struggles. Be grateful for the people who are doing more than you. They can show you what's truly possible.

Your job as an entrepreneur is to never let yourself settle. Always expand yourself in every way, including the quality of your relationships. It's not just about who is making the most money. That's not always the best determinant of success, though it can be a very clear one. It's very likely there are people who you can look up to who are doing more in their family life, their love life, or their spiritual life.

Remember, we are all just people who are the product of our choices. The choices we make are massively impacted by our beliefs about what is possible, and our beliefs about what is possible are massively impacted by the people we surround ourselves with. There is no shortest route to success, but the world is full of people who can show you where to turn if you're willing to listen.

Chapter 6

Are You Ready for Success?

Are you ready for success? If all the success you dream about, wish for, and are so hungry for came today, would it all come crashing down around you because you are not truly ready?

Are you ready to capitalize on all the additional positive externalities that come from getting a big win? Do you have the right team in place? Do you have all the resources you might need? Have you built the right network of people who can support you?

Do you have the mental endurance required to do something not only great but extraordinary? Do you have the discipline and organizational skills you're going to need to be able to capitalize fully on a big win?

Chances are, you don't. And that is fine. Each and every one of us, including myself, is always growing more and more ready for more success by the day. You don't need to rush. Instead, you need to know everything you do and experience in your life is somehow, whether you see it or not, contributing to your ability to succeed at a higher level in the future.

Even when you experience failure, you are stacking bricks to build the foundation your eventual success will be built on. I tried so many different business ideas for eight years straight before I had my first big breakthrough. I was desperate for success.

I tasted some success when I was twenty-two. I made almost a million dollars with my concert promotion company. But back then, I was not ready for success, and I ended up losing all my money in one night, and on top of that, I got sued for another $250,000. All the money I made the previous year, I lost. I couldn't even afford a lawyer to protect myself from the lawsuit filed against me.

This might sound like an awful situation to be in, and it was at the time. But looking back, I can actually say it's the best thing that's ever happened to me. Let me explain why.

After losing all my money and getting sued (to make matters worse, by one of my friends), I was at a very low point. All the positive beliefs and visions of expansive possibility I had built up in my head came crashing down. I didn't come from a background that guaranteed success by any means. Where I came from, success was virtually impossible.

But by making a few key moves that worked out to my advantage, my belief in myself started to become more real to me than the beliefs of other people in my environment. I don't know which was harder for me to go through at the time— losing all my money or losing my belief in myself.

When you're twenty-two, flat broke, with no business or income, and you're getting sued for $250,000, that's pretty much rock fucking bottom. Maybe even lower than that, if such a state is possible.

I know it sounds insane to say that was the best thing that's ever happened to me, but it's true. If that hadn't happened, I would not be on the path I'm on now where I'm able to help and inspire other people to take control of their own lives.

I learned a giant lesson going through all that. Having a $250,000 lawsuit on your hands when you're twenty-two is extremely stressful, but it seasoned me. It gave me the grit and the willpower I needed to have in order to stand up and fight for my future. On top of that, it made my other problems seem not so huge.

A lot of us get very stressed out about little problems. Getting stressed out about small problems paralyzes us. But when you go through a huge problem in your life or business, your mental muscles tear down. You have no other choice at that point but to build them back up to be even stronger than before.

The mental muscles I built up going through that extremely hard time now defend me from stress every day. Now, whenever I am faced with an everyday-sized problem, I see it as a little fly, and I can swat it away. I can take care of it and make it disappear as fast as it arrived without expending all of my energy.

Think about it this way. If you've had a little bit of success, but it's been overshadowed by some bigger failures in your life, you now have valuable experience you can use to your advantage on your journey to win. I don't believe anyone can develop the inner mental game required to succeed at a highlevel unless they experience the pain of failure.

When failure happens, something inside of you changes. Your killer instincts kick in, and your evolutionary will to survive rises to the surface. You could be the most passive, peaceful person in the world, but when this happens to you, watch out! That's some intense energy about to be released, and if it's used properly, it can be the catalyst for the major breakthrough you've been looking for.

You don't need to rush this process. Your time will come.

At twenty-eight, when I had my first big win in e-commerce, I was much more prepared for success. I was much smarter. I was also driven by deeper motivations than I was at twenty-two. It wasn't all about partying, making money, and impressing other people anymore. I had more knowledge, and I knew more what to do with it. I had a better sense of the direction I wanted my life to go, and my life was much more balanced. I had a level head.

So, when my first big win in e-commerce happened, I didn't get overwhelmed, and I didn't go crazy and blow all my money on stupid stuff. I was smart, and I was poised. My only thought was, "Okay, what can I do next? How can I capitalize on this?" This allowed me to build multiple businesses afterwards because I now had the network I needed, and I knew both what I should and shouldn't do.

I'm not where I will be in ten years, and I'm not where I will be in twenty years either. If you look at massive businesses like Tesla or Virgin—building a business like one of these requires a whole different level of readiness for success; a level I don't possess right now. But I know that given time, I will get there.

I'm continuing to be on my journey, and I know that. I'm happy to be on it, and I'm sticking to the plan every single day. Just remember, it does not have to happen today, and it will happen.

When I was young and naïve about business, I wasn't very emotionally intelligent. I was prone to looking at the numbers and either becoming very excited or very upset, very easily. This problem is widespread among beginner entrepreneurs, but there's an even worse and more common problem which I also fell into—not looking at my numbers at all.

Whatever you do, don't do this. Know your expenses. Know your revenue. Know your profit, and definitely learn how to figure out what you're going to have to pay in taxes. If you don't pay your taxes, you won't be in business very long. You'd be surprised how many people just starting out in business don't think about this until it's too late. Not knowing this stuff can bankrupt you, so pay attention.

If numbers aren't your first language, get someone in your network that excels in this area. When I was just getting started in business, like most people, I had no clue what I needed to know, and I also didn't know who the best people were to ask for help from.

For a long time, I didn't have the right accountant keeping track of my numbers, the right designers working for me, or the right website developers to keep up with what I was trying to do. On top of that, I wasn't self-aware enough to realize I was running my business off of a cliff by not taking care of these foundational pieces to my business.

I didn't know I needed to be proactive instead of reactive, and the balance in my life was way off. I never took the time to think about what was coming next or to think strategically about my next move. In some ways, this played to my advantage because I got a lot of stuff done all the time. I was always in a "go, go, go" mindset.

But now that I know better and have more experience, I'm able to use my ability to grind for what I want *after* deciding what I should logically be working on next, instead of just running from one place to another and staying busy.

When I was younger, I pushed hard, and I did well, but I was also spending a lot of money. I hustled, and I enjoyed the success I did achieve, but I wasn't ready for it. My failure hurt, but it didn't kill me. Now it's just a part of my journey that I've learned from, and hopefully you can learn from it too.

My next successful venture was with a company I created called Glidr. With this company, I was one of the first two people to bring hoverboards to the United States. In our first month, we did over $250,000 in sales. I was able to achieve this because of all I had learned from promoting concerts. I knew how to get things in front of people and how to make money.

One of the things I did to promote Glidr was forge a bunch of relationships with different influencers and celebrities to promote our product. But because we sold so many products so fast, things started to get crazy. We had more orders than we could handle, and we were importing the products ourselves and then shipping them out. We honestly didn't know what we were doing. Hoverboards were constantly getting caught up at customs, and customers were getting angry.

The quality of the hoverboards started to become inconsistent because we didn't have a good system in place to do quality control. Still, the rapid sales growth we experienced right off the bat was enough to catch the eye of Mark Cuban, who called me personally to tell me he was interested in my brand.

However, the conversation with Mark was not able to develop because the final nail in the coffin for Glidr was just around the corner. We didn't have a patent on the product. The company which did have a patent on the product was going to sue us if we didn't stop selling hoverboards. They would have easily won the lawsuit. We were forced to shut down the business.

You have no idea how much that sucked, but in the end, it turned out to be yet another win. It showed me, again, what I didn't know. I didn't know how to source products, do quality control, and still get them to customers within a reasonable time frame. And nobody I was working with had any kind of logistical experience they could bring to the table.

I also knew nothing about patent law, and I didn't have an attorney who did. I wasn't ready for success in all the ways I needed to be, but what I did have on my side was a willingness to do anything in order to be successful.

71

Looking back, it makes sense why things didn't develop further than they did. The biggest lesson I learned is, in business, you can't do anything big on your own. You need to have a solid team around you. The idea of the self-mademan is a myth. That doesn't mean success doesn't start with personal responsibility. It means you have to know how to work with others, be willing to give credit where it is due, and become a well-respected person.

To attract a team of A-players, you have to be one yourself. You have to be a good communicator, first and foremost. You have to be able to communicate your vision to other people, and you have to be able to motivate and inspire other people. To inspire others, you have to be inspired yourself.

Even then, it takes time to build the right team and the right network. For example, I hired fourteen different accountants before I found the one I work with now. All fourteen of the previous accountants were okay, but they were not exceptional. They weren't proactive. They just did the bare minimum. It is true that in business you are only as good as your weakest link. Everyone has to see the overall vision, want to get there together, and want to share in the rewards that come from doing great work. Diligence is an important trait to develop in yourself and in your team.

If I had started a $100 million company without the right support system around me, I probably would have learned some serious lessons or failed quickly. It's important to look for people who want to work with you long-term. As you gain more traction, and as you become more respected as a person, many people will reach out to you and want to work with you on different deals. Then your challenge changes from having to inspire people to want to work with you, to needing to know how to vet people to see if they're worth your time.

I receive a hundred messages a day from different people online. Fifteen of these messages are usually business opportunities. And of these fifteen, about two of them actually sound like good opportunities. But still, that doesn't mean they are worth pursuing right now. You have to compare the opportunities you come across to how they relate to your greater vision. If they don't fit, or if they don't feel right, it's better to say no than to do something you don't believe in.

Being a leader and entrepreneur is not all about how much money you make now or how successful your businesses have been in the past. It all starts with the fundamentals of being a good person. You have to be someone other people can look up to. You have to be sincere, and you have to be genuine. If you don't start with these basics, no one you want to work with will stick around very long.

That's why this book is focused on helping you develop yourself as a whole person and not just as a businessperson. Everything you do and everything you are in life plays a massive role in your ability to inspire others to rally around your vision and bring their best to the game of business every single day. There is no line between your normal life and your entrepreneurial life. If one or the other is not in order, it will eventually drag everything down.

All of my experiences in life and in business have prepared me for where I am now. At the time of this writing, my team is made up of forty-nine people. When I first started, I did everything I could by myself. Then I hired someone to come in and handle all the daily routine tasks like customer support emails, phone calls, live chat, and Facebook messages.

The next hire I made was somebody to do my other daily tasks that require a higher level of skill. This meant hiring somebody to run my ads who understood the platform I was using, and I showed them the rules to follow to make sure my ads continued to function at the same level in terms of spend and profit.

This allowed me to generate more money for the business than before, even though I now had the additional costs of paying others to work with me. My business was at a point where the more time I could free up for me to create and strategize, the faster the business could grow.

Then, as I made more money, more opportunities came my way, and it was time to expand my business both vertically and horizontally. So, I hired somebody to be my right-hand man for a small salary, and I included high incentive-based compensation and a beautiful place to live as part of the deal as well.

This allowed me to act as a mentor and invest in another leader in my business who was able to take on the entrepreneurial mindset and start building out other facets of my business right alongside me. As the business continued to grow, we diversified and broke into new areas such as education and technology.

This growth and expansion required more support, development, and sales people. We worked to build these different teams up, and once they grew to about ten people each, management and leadership roles were delegated for each of them. I found this to be a very effective strategy.

I know a lot of entrepreneurs worry they won't be able to build a solid team. That's why I've just explained, step by step, how I've been able to do it successfully. The biggest thing you need to know is you don't have to rush, and you also don't have to look for people who have the most experience unless you're hiring someone for a very specific task.

It's more important to judge the character of a person before you hire them than to judge their work experience, especially if you want to build a young team that can grow with you into the future. You will have different qualities that are important to you based on your business and your future goals, but what I look for is somebody who wants to win, first and foremost.

I don't want to work with anybody who is just in it for a paycheck. I don't want to work with anybody who is just out to see what they can get for themselves. I want people who are open-minded, versatile, and focused on helping everybody win together.

If I'm considering hiring someone, and the first question out of their mouth is, "What are you going to pay me?" I'm not interested. Anybody that's looking to just get paid more than their last job is not going to be a good fit. I don't make decisions for my businesses based solely on how much money I can produce in the shortest amount of time, and I don't want that to be an employee's focus either.

I want long-term profits because those add up to more over time anyway, and I want long-term relationships with the people who work with me so we can continue to work on the vision together and enjoy watching everything grow.

I want people on my team who can say, "I love this, and I'm willing to do anything and everything to make it succeed." I will hire somebody with that attitude and no experience every time, over somebody who has a lot of experience but just does their work because it gives them a paycheck.

The life of an entrepreneur and a leader is not always glorious. It's a lot harder to be an entrepreneur than it is to be an employee. The benefits and freedom can be great as an entrepreneur, but the pressure and stress can be greater. As an employee, you just have to do the work required. You have to put in some time. You have to do the tasks at hand and show up when you say you're going to show up. That's the minimum.

As an entrepreneur, you always have to be growing. You can't just do the minimum, because there is no minimum. Once you stop growing, you become obsolete, and you die. It's a never-ending cycle of growth, failure, and success as an entrepreneur, until, of course, you sell your business and do whatever the hell you want. But when you own your own business, it's a forever thing. There is no forty-hour workweek and two weeks' paid vacation. Nobody is guaranteeing you any money, and you might lose it all at some point.

If there's something that needs to be done, and you're in bed at 2:00 a.m. when you remember it, you have to wake up and take care of it. You can never turn off as an entrepreneur. Your business is the first thing you think about when you wake up, and it's the first thing you think about when you go to bed. In fact, I feel guilty if I sit down and watch a movie and turn my mind off from thinking about my business.

I'm not saying that's good or necessary, but it's what happens when the livelihood of your business and your employees depends on you. So, you have to know how to deal with that. You have to make the conscious decision to remain balanced because balance will never come about by accident for an entrepreneur.

There is always room for constant improvement in every way. There is always a way to become a better leader for your team. There is always a higher standard you can hold yourself to. As an entrepreneur, you want to live in discomfort, so you never relax and fall behind.

The average person looks for comfort in every area of life. The average person can get another job if they have to. They say to themselves, "I could have my own business someday, maybe," but they never try because it's too much work. They work for the weekends that blow past them in the blink of an eye, and on Sunday night they're dreading Monday morning.

Every entrepreneur's favorite day is Monday because that's the day of the week where they're most hungry for more and are ready to go get it. If you want to work eight hours a day, go home, not think about work, and spend the evening doing whatever you feel like, that's fine. But that's not going to prepare you for success at the highest level.

If you yearn to be a successful entrepreneur, just know it gets harder as you go. It does not get easier. If you want to have sustained success, it's going to require consistent hard work and discipline. You are going to have to know how to come up with a plan, and then stick to it.

You will never wake up in the morning and feel like saying, "Today is the day I become an entrepreneur." Even if you do say this, and you mean it, and you take the action required to make this true, the rewards won't come immediately.

Yes, your life can change overnight, but all the years before a massive breakthrough are even more important. The days when nobody believes in you, and even your belief in yourself is rocked from time to time–those are the days that prepare you for success.

The people who do well in this game are the people who love every minute of pain they have to endure to get to the top. So, let me ask you again. Are you ready for success?

Chapter 7

Who Not to
Take Advice From

As a beginner, the first day I decided I was going to become an entrepreneur, everybody wanted to give me their opinion. My mom told me for four years straight, every time I talked to her, that I needed to get a job.

I'd tell her about my business plans, but she couldn't see them working out because she had never created a business herself. To her, it wasn't possible. She had limiting beliefs about the entrepreneurial journey.

Every time I told her about my plans, she would say, "I wish the best for you, from your mouth to God's ears." Every time I told her about a good idea I had, she said that, and I hated it.

I would tell her I was just going to go for it. And she'd say, "Yes, I'm hopeful for you, but you need to get a job. You cannot *not* get a job." After hearing this so many times, it started to become ingrained in my head, and I started believing it. If something was going wrong in my business, this thought popped into my head, and it caused me to question myself at times.

Still, there was another part of me that thought, "I know I don't need to get a job. I know I can do this."

I love my mom unconditionally, but I have realized there is certain advice I should take from her, and there is some I should ignore. Since she isn't an entrepreneur, I shouldn't look to her for entrepreneurial advice. That doesn't make sense.

Maybe you've had a similar experience with your parents or other people in your family. It's not that these people don't want the best for you. They obviously do. It's just that everyone can only give advice based on what they've experienced. If someone hasn't experienced success in business for themselves, then you shouldn't expect them to lead you towards that path for yourself.

Even people who genuinely care about your well-being could want you to fail. No, not because they don't want what's good for you, but rather because they don't want to think that the choices they've made for themselves were wrong. If you took the risk that they weren't willing to take, they want to be able to give themselves a pat on the back for not taking the risk that caused you to collapse.

If you often talk about your plans and ideas with people who aren't in business for themselves, you are going to get exposed to their limiting beliefs. If you tell them something off-hand like, "I'm thinking about opening up an office in Los Angeles," instead of speaking from experience or just saying nothing, they will likely form a snap judgment of what they think of your idea and share it with you.

Typically, unless the person you're talking to is a very positive person, they will probably say something like, "Oh, are you sure? I don't know if you want to do that. Taxes are really high in California. It's probably not worth it."

Whatever someone says to you, it could be accurate, or it could be not accurate at all. Either way, other people's opinions aren't to be taken as the truth unless they can back them up with experience.

In this example, if the person immediately puts down your idea of opening up an office in California, it's possible they've never even been there before. Or it could be they've never thought about opening an office anywhere, either in California or anywhere else. That means they haven't actually looked to see if there could be a solution to a problem like high taxes.

The moral of the story is you don't want to listen to people who have limiting beliefs and no experience. Unless you are learning from someone who has done exactly what you want to do, then you're hurting yourself by listening to other people who want to give you nothing but warnings and reasons why you can't do something off the top of their head.

When it comes to hard decisions in life, sometimes you just have to listen to yourself and do what you think is right. If you pay attention to yourself and what you believe is right, most of the time you're going to make the best decision for you, even if it doesn't make perfect logical sense.

If you try to consider opinions from too many sources with every decision you make, you will develop decision paralysis. You're better off making one hundred decisions this month than not making a single decision, even if sixty of them are wrong decisions. If only forty are right, you are still much, much closer than you would be having made no decision at all.

If you don't believe me, take it from Elon Musk who said, "It is better to make many decisions per unit time with a slightly higher error rate, than few with a slightly lower error rate, because obviously one of your future right decisions can be to reverse an earlier wrong one, provided the earlier one was not catastrophic, which they rarely are."

The best thing you can do when you are faced with a difficult decision is to not let it overwhelm you. Quick decision makers always get to the right answer faster than people who don't make any decisions at all. It is always best to keep moving forward. If you do this, you will almost always arrive at a place you didn't expect, and there's a good chance it will be a place that's even better than what you expected.

Where you end up after making a decision is almost never worse than what you expected because our brains are naturally very good at giving us the worst-case scenario by default. This is because our entire biological system is rigged to protect us from pain.

In the modern world, in most cases, the pain we experience from making a wrong decision is never fatal. In the past, doing something wrong could have gotten you killed or excommunicated from your tribe, and our brains evolved to protect us from making wrong decisions because the stakes were actually that high back then.

But if you can train yourself to not be so affected by the emotional pain that may come from making a wrong decision, you can free yourself from this biological prison and, if you have to, fail your way to success *like every other successful person on earth has ever done.*

Waiting. Not making a decision. Getting a second opinion. Getting a third opinion. Getting a fourth opinion. Talking to everyone, even if they haven't done what you want to do—all this is unnecessary, and most of the time it will just hurt you when you are just starting out as an entrepreneur.

In the beginning, you may not even have access to people that have the right answers to your questions. You might only have access to people who think they know the answers, but typically the people who are most willing to provide their opinion to you are the people you should listen to the least.

This happens all the time in various Facebook groups. Someone, a beginner entrepreneur, goes into a business-themed Facebook group to ask a question because they are feeling uncertain of themselves, and they have to make a decision. They don't know who to ask in their network because they barely have one, so they are stuck with either following their gut, Googling for hours, or getting an answer from somebody in a Facebook group.

Now, I'm not saying Facebook groups aren't useful. We use one to help our students. But if a beginner entrepreneur goes into a random, free Facebook group and they ask a question, they're just asking to be pointed in the wrong direction by people who know nothing about business but spend all their time sharing their opinions in groups.

You have to consider the source of the advice you get when it comes to your business, your health, and any other area of your life. If the source is solid, the advice is likely solid. If you can't determine if the source is solid, don't take the advice.

I'm not trying to say there is no good information online for free. There is tons of good and positive information online for the beginner entrepreneur. Books are even better, and they cost almost nothing. Reading books like this one can totally change your perspective and help you in a major way, and that's the reason I wrote this one.

Just becoming aware of how others have developed themselves over time, built successful businesses, and gone on to achieve massive success can help you break past whatever limiting beliefs you hold to be true about yourself in a major way. YouTube and countless other websites give access to tons of helpful information, but the key is what you do with it and how you integrate it into your overall plan.

That's why I teach my students exactly what I do and have done to create success in e-commerce for myself over and over again. When you have a specific plan to follow that was created by somebody who has already traveled the road you want to travel, this gives you a better chance of succeeding at a much faster rate than if you had to piece all of the details together on your own.

If you want to learn the specifics of the business you're interested in starting for yourself, at some point, you will have to invest in learning from others. And I highly suggest investing in learning from somebody who is the best at what they do, and not just somebody who teaches something they learned from somebody else but doesn't practice what they preach.

Again, you have to start by expanding your belief in what is possible in whatever way possible, then go looking for the details and specifics only an expert can reveal to you. This is the most efficient and productive way to go about developing not only yourself but also your business.

Start building the foundation for all of your success in the beginning however you can. Find what resonates with you. Get yourself into a good mindset, and keep yourself there by not introducing all kinds of contradictory opinions and ideas into it. Fortify your foundation so it can hold the massive weight of expert opinion later on, so you can continue to build your business larger and larger once it's off the ground.

Take a word of advice from someone who has been there and done that. When you are first starting out as an entrepreneur, you need to *not* talk to the people around you about what you're doing. If you talk about it all the time, that's going to open up a windfall of conversation, even justifiable conversation, with people who don't believe you can succeed, simply because you haven't yet.

They're technically not wrong in doubting you, either. Because when you first start, and you have no results to speak of, you technically haven't done anything yet. But your focus has to be on what you can do, almost to the point where you are willfully delusional and believe you're already successful.

Most people are not okay with that unless they've been in your shoes before. So, honestly, just don't talk about what you're doing in the beginning. It's not a good use of your time. In a very real sense, you don't have energy to waste on talk anyways. Starting a business is like pushing a boulder uphill.

Eventually, you will reach the top, and then things will start rolling down the other side. But in the beginning, it requires a lot of energy to keep things moving uphill.

A lot of people these days want to get on social media and build a huge fan base for their imaginary business by talking all the time about what they're going to do and repeating all the same motivational phrases as all the gurus out there. I'm not saying it's bad to inspire other people, but make sure you have the results for yourself before you try to help other people. The time to inspire and motivate will come, but it almost never comes first.

Keep your work to yourself and work on it in private until you have some results worth showing people. You're going to be doubting yourself the whole way, and that's fine, but you don't need other people to add to that doubt.

In one of the most well-respected self-development books of all time, *The 7 Habits of Highly Effective People*, author Stephen Covey says, "Private victories precede public victories. You can't invert that process any more than you can harvest a crop before you plant it."

If you do the things I've taught you in this book, and stay quiet about it, you will achieve many private victories. You will break through your subconscious standards, push past your limiting beliefs, discipline yourself, and be ready to capitalize on your wins to create compounding success.

However, if you are focused on talk, other people are going to talk back to you. In most cases, what they say won't be all that encouraging. If you internalize advice from a bad source, the outcome is also likely to be bad. This is why you must take action in private to start.

Expand your personal beliefs so negative talk simply bounces off of you. Get to the point where you know what people say about you is more of a reflection of their own insecurities than anything you are doing right or wrong. Allow people to doubt you, because they're going to do so no matter what level of success you attain.

Even Amazon's Jeff Bezos is scrutinized, and he's the richest man on earth because he provides the most value to others. There is no way to escape the negative opinion of others, except to build such a firm internal belief in yourself that external opinions no longer matter to you.

Protect your time and protect your energy from outside influences that aren't positive, because even if you start a business with all the motivation in the world, eventually that's going to go away. Even if you go to events, surround yourself with the right people, read books, invest in your education, and have success, there will be times when you will not feel like doing anything to keep raising the bar.

You can't have discipline if you don't believe it will get you anywhere better than where you are at right now. And when it comes to business, complacency is the hospital room where successful entrepreneurs go to die a slow and painful death.

But if you can discipline yourself to make minimal improvement every single day, you will keep complacency at bay. Not only that, you will end up miles ahead of everyone else who only attempts to grow when the potential reward is greater than the pain of trying to change.

You have to be willing to take small steps. Small steps create small results, but small results compound over time to make a huge difference. I urge you to dedicate yourself to taking small steps everyday and not getting discouraged when you see other people taking bigger ones.

Think of the process of starting a business as similar to starting a fire by rubbing two sticks together. At first, you will only get a little spark. But that spark has the potential to light a massive fire that can keep you warm and cook your food.

But if you aren't disciplined, and instead you start talking to people, listening to negative opinions, going back

85

and forth, and wasting your energy, that's like throwing water on your fire. If you've only got a small flame, it doesn't take much water to put it out completely.

Once your fire is roaring, believe me when I say people are going to be attracted to it like moths. Then, no matter what you do or say, people are going to come along and start throwing big glasses of water on your flame. But you know what? At this point, that's not going to change a damn thing. People can say what they want, and it won't affect you at all.

When you are just getting started, you are trying to build up your power. Every time you go out and talk to people about what you're doing, you're releasing a little bit of that power you're trying to build up. You're giving it away to people for nothing.

But when you keep things to yourself, you are concentrating your power in one place. You're keeping your energy focused in one spot. Eventually, your power is going to become so concentrated that there is no way that when you release it in the right direction, it won't produce the massive result you're looking for.

Just remember, actions speak louder than words. That's not a new phrase, but it's a true one.

Now, I'm not saying all this stuff just because it sounds good. I practiced this philosophy myself when I was working on growing my drop-shipping business to $50,000 a day.

When my drop-shipping business went from doing $2,000 the first day to $7,000 the next, my first thought was, "Wow, I've never made $7,000 in revenue in one day before. This is awesome!" I saw there was some power behind what I was doing, so I kept at it.

The next day, I went from $7,000 to $14,000. I hadn't told anyone about the jump from $2,000 to $7,000 the day before, and now I wanted to call up everybody I knew and tell them what had happened.

But I thought to myself, "No, Jared, just shut up. Don't tell anyone about this. Just keep doing what you're doing." I knew if I started talking, people were going to start giving me their ideas and opinions, and if I started listening to them, there was a chance I could mess up what was already working. So, I made myself keep my mouth shut.

On the third day, I went from $14,000 to $35,000 in revenue. Two days later, it jumped up to $50,000, and I profited $20,000 in a single day. I could hardly believe it. My standards and beliefs were completely blown away.

Before this, I knew it was possible to make money like this, but it wasn't my reality. When it happened, I was extremely grateful, and I decided if it stopped happening, I wouldn't be resentful.

For two months steady, revenue stayed at around $50,000 a day, and I didn't tell anyone what was going on. Over this time period, the reality of it started to become very real to me. I realized things were not slowing down, so I finally began to share what had happened with other people.

When I shared the story, I noticed everyone started to look at me differently. I wasn't just a naïve dude who wouldn't take a job and get back to reality. Now I had done something right. But at the same time, I knew I was the same person, with much of the same knowledge I had been working to acquire for a long time.

To other people, it may have looked like overnight success. But to me, it was just the result of a lot of hard work, a lot of refusing to be told I couldn't do it, and years of trial and error. That's how I made it happen, and that's how you can make it happen for yourself too.

Keep yourself grounded. Stay stable. Stay focused. Don't waste your time and energy on talk. Let your results speak for themselves, and know who *not* to take advice from.

Chapter 8

How to See Clearly

When your mind is quiet, you can see things clearly. When you can see clearly, you have a better chance for success. If you are stressed, anxious, or depressed, it's difficult to make good choices because these states of mind make it very difficult to tap into your own intuition. Many people don't even believe intuition exists because they have never stopped and given themselves the mental space to experience it.

Intuition doesn't get talked about a lot by business people because it sounds almost magical, but we have all experienced intuition at some point in our lives. Intuition is the feeling you get in your stomach when you're about to make a business deal with somebody, and although the deal makes perfect logical sense, you just don't feel good about it.

It's also the feeling you get in your gut when you come up with an idea that everybody else around you says is crazy, but you know is going to work. Intuition is linked to your self-confidence in a very direct way because being able to capitalize on it requires a high degree of trust in yourself.

Now, it's not true that all the feelings you experience in life are going to point you in the right direction. But with practice, and by setting up the right conditions in your life, you can begin to learn for yourself how intuition can give you an advantage in business.

Listening to your intuition is not a scientific process, but that doesn't mean it's not important or useful. In fact, Albert Einstein himself said, "All great achievements of science must start from intuitive knowledge. At times I feel certain I am right while not knowing the reason."

To understand intuition, you must first understand there are two parts of the mind. There is the conscious mind, and there is the subconscious mind. The subconscious mind does not "think" in language, but it is constantly gathering data from our environment and our experiences without us even knowing it. In fact, neuroscientists have found that ninety-five to ninety-nine percent of what we do every day is controlled by the subconscious mind.

The intuition we have about certain things comes from our subconscious mind, based on information it has gathered from our environment and experience we are not consciously aware of. If you look at intuition from this perspective, it does not have to be thought of as a mystical thing. It also explains why our intuition is often so accurate, even when we don't understand its conclusions—there is a lot going on in our lives the conscious mind can't take in and process, but which the more powerful subconscious mind can.

Everyone's subconscious mind is taking in data, processing it, and producing intuition on a regular basis. The problem is most people spend all of their time listening more to what their conscious mind is telling them, as it continuously runs calculations and makes interpretations with useful, but limited information. Not many people know how to hear their subconscious intuition when it speaks.

The best way to make space to listen to your subconscious intuition is to clean up your physical environment and get yourself organized. If you have clutter all over the place, that's nearly the same as having clutter all over your mind. A clean environment, however, produces a clear mind.

Good organization is the foundation of all success. And it's not just things at the office (if you have one) that need to be in order. It starts at home. If your closet, bedroom, bathroom, living room, and kitchen are all a huge mess, and you're trying to build a business, you're just creating more challenges for yourself, even if you don't realize it.

If you need to find something as simple as a piece of pen and paper, and you can't do that when you need to, you're setting yourself up to fail. You can also forget about finding a way to produce a massively successful business if you can't find the right file on your computer when somebody asks you for it. If you can't find basic things when you need them, you're obstructing your flow. And without flow, you can't access the intuitive knowledge necessary to do anything great.

But if everything is tidy, and you know exactly where everything goes and where to find it, you don't even have to think about simple things like finding a pen and paper anymore. Your subconscious will direct you when you need to get these things, and you can stay fully absorbed in your work.

This allows you start a massive project, develop it from its infancy stage, and turn it into a full-blown masterpiece. Flow enables creativity, and organization enables flow. If you're inhibiting your flow, then your ideas and creative projects will never come to full fruition. But when you setup your environment in such a way so that it doesn't obstruct your flow, you create the space for success to be incubated.

I know some of you reading this are terrified right now. You might be thinking, "Organization is not on my list of skills." And that's totally normal for anyone who considers themselves creative. I'm not an organized person at all by nature.

If you're not an organized person by nature, that's okay. You don't have to be. Remember, as an entrepreneur, your job is to never stay stuck in one place. You have to always be growing. And one area you can grow in, no matter how horrible you are at it right now, is organization.

Organization requires nothing more and nothing less than discipline. It's just a matter of, "Do I want to get up and put this thing in the right place or am I just going to throw it here, in this pile?" That is a very simple choice with a very clear answer. The more you make the right choice when questions like that pop into your mind, the more organized you will become.

It's common for very intelligent people to be not very organized. When this is the case, they convince themselves that if organization doesn't come to them naturally, that's just the way it's always going to be. But organization doesn't have to feel natural to you. You just have to do it. It will become natural the more you practice it, just like everything else in life.

Eventually, you will get to the point where you can't stand to have things out of place because you will be able to immediately sense the way it disrupts your mental state. The Chinese concept of FengShui, which you've probably heard of before, suggests a cluttered house leads to a cluttered mind. And a cluttered mind leads only to bad decision-making. I've experienced this personally.

The big reason why my first concert promotion business failed was because of my lack of organization. I was living in a penthouse apartment, and my shit was everywhere. I was traveling all the time. I wasn't keeping organized records of my expenses. I was always flying by the seat of my pants and trying to power my way through everything. I didn't take any time to get organized.

Using only my mental memory, I tried to remember travel dates, DJ lineups, and rider requests for tons of different artists. I didn't know my numbers at all or even where to find them if I needed to. That is absolutely the worst thing you can do when you're trying to run a successful business. Human beings are incredibly forgetful. We don't remember stuff very well, and it doesn't matter how smart you are; you're not the exception.

If you are managing something complex, as any business is bound to be, then you have to keep organized records of everything. The full extent of my organizational skills when I was just getting started in business was occasionally writing to-do lists of things I had to get done and checking them off. But even then, I did this on random scraps of paper I'd put in random places and would then lose all over my apartment. I didn't even think to have anyone help with that stuff either, because I didn't know it was important.

But now you do. If you need help organizing things because they're out of control already, hire somebody to help you. It will be worth it. It could save you from making a huge mistake in your business.

My lack of organization led to my downfall in the concert promotion industry. You know the story well now. I booked a huge show without knowing any of the details I needed to know, lost all my money, and got sued on top of that. Had I kept my life and business organized, I'm confident I wouldn't have made such a bad decision.

I'm also confident that if you improve your organizational skills even one percent, you will see an increase your creative ability. Any increase in creative ability can make a huge impact on the success of your business. Creativity is what drives innovation, and innovation, even in small amounts, is highly prized in business.

For example, Apple didn't invent the smartphone, but they did innovate it to create the iPhone, which has now been called one of the most profitable products in history. Apple is constantly coming up with creative and imaginative products, and so are all the other big players.

Amazon is working on drones to drop off packages. They're also figuring out how to ship products to people before they've even ordered them based on their customer data. That's new. That's exciting. That's going to draw attention to their brand, even if the idea fails.

Being creative and imaginative has huge benefits in business. Even when an experiment fails, if it's done right, it doesn't have to sink a business, and it can keep progress moving forward. But look at companies like Kmart who, in the past, had the knowledge and ability required to run a department store successfully. They did great for a while, but they kept the same business model and continued to use the same old practices. Now they're literally dying.

At the individual level, it's important feed your creativity by doing things that open up your creative mind. That might be painting, playing the guitar, playing the piano, singing, dancing, writing, or cooking, whatever you enjoy doing. Any of these kinds of things will keep your creative mind flowing, even if you only do them once a week. Pepper these things into your routine, and the creative moments you experience while doing them will translate into your daily life and business, helping you think outside of the box.

Steve Jobs said, "It is in Apple's DNA that technology alone is not enough—it's technology married with liberal arts, married with the humanities, that yields us the results that make our heart sing." I take this to mean that everything in our lives influences what we do, the products we sell, and the businesses we build.

It doesn't matter what industry you're in; at some level, you have to create something people care about. You can't do that without creativity, because without it, you are just giving people the same old thing they've seen before, in the same old way.

Creativity allows you to look at ordinary, everyday objects and re-imagine them in a way that makes them even more valuable to your clients or customers. To do this, you have to be able to access and understand all the information that's available to you, from your intuitive feelings to the trends in data. Without this ability, trying to run a business is like trying to sail a boat through a storm without a lighthouse to warn you where land lies. You might be able to do okay for a little while, but wouldn't you rather see things clearly and avoid a crash?

Chapter 9

Get Started!

When you're just starting out with any new project, it's normal to have a vision of what you want the finished product to look like when it's complete. This is good to have, but it can also hold you back. If your vision is perfection, this can keep you from getting started out of fear you're not going to hit the mark you've set for yourself.

This fear leads to excuses for why you're not working on the project because you can never guarantee perfection. Without a guarantee of perfection, some people convince themselves it must not be the right time to do anything at all. But if you wait until you have everything figured out to start, you will never create anything.

That's why it's always better to just start doing things, even if you're not sure how it's going to work out. As a general rule in life and business, nothing ever works out exactly as you expected it to anyway. The good news is, a lot of times, things work out *better* than you expected.

Getting started is always the first step. Once you get in motion, the details typically take care of themselves. If you just get started, you will end up in a better place than your starting point every single time.

The process of creating something great is never linear, especially if you're doing something you've never done before. There will be twists and turns, and the whole experience will be full of both unexpected challenges and exciting surprises. Always remember perfection does not exist, and creating anything is better than creating nothing at all in every case.

A good example from my own life is when I had the idea to build a software that would help people find winning products they could sell and drop-ship online. At first, I didn't even know how to start or who I should ask for help. I figured I would need a designer, a few project managers, and a team of developers, but I didn't know those people, and I wasn't sure how to find them.

So, for a while, I just did nothing, but I quickly realized none of this stuff was going to figure itself out for me, so I decided to just go for it. I found a software development team based in India who I thought could handle the project, even if the result wasn't going to be as perfect as if I had hired and groomed my own team. I decided to let go of the end result, put the team to the task, and let them build the software based on my instructions. The surprising thing was it wasn't as expensive or hard for them to build the software as I had expected.

And while I wouldn't say it's perfect, this simple software now has over ten thousand users on it, and it has helped people produce millions of dollars in sales. So, that's the direct benefit of having created this software, but even more indirect benefits have come out of having built it as well.

This software has opened up tons of indirect opportunities and allowed me to build some amazing relationships I know will play a huge role in the future of my businesses. There are all kinds of indirect positive benefits that come from just doing things. And there is absolutely zero benefit to standing on the sidelines and watching everybody else take action.

When you are a person who gets things done and brings ideas to life, even if what you produce is not perfect, you will attract people to you who are also out there creating things and taking action. As an entrepreneur, you can never produce perfection on your own or on your first try, but as you complete more work, you continually attract the right people into your life who you can join forces with.

People who create things like other people who create things and have good follow-through. Being a person who creates and follows through is way more important than being a person who comes up with great ideas, but never gets them off the ground.

Some of the most common reasons people give for not doing something they want to do are, "There is too much competition" or "It's just way too hard to break into that industry." Has anyone ever said either of those things to you? Have you ever said either of those two things to somebody else? There is no doubt in my mind you've heard this stuff said or something similar, and typically the people who say it are people who haven't even tried to do what they're saying is too hard.

But if everybody thinks something is too hard, so they just give up before even trying, what does that mean for you if you are willing to be an action taker? It means there is hardly any competition because *most of your competition has already given up.* All you have to do is keep grinding away.

If I had to boil success down to one simple formula, it would be this: *think less, do more.* Ideas that die on the vine end up killing the whole plant. Your first business, product, or service doesn't even have to be significantly better than the competition's on your first try. That doesn't mean you can settle for mediocrity. What it means is once you've got something–anything–then you can improve it. You can't improve upon something that doesn't even exist.

Over thinking is the enemy of creation. People hold themselves back so much by over thinking things that don't matter. For example, they might want to build a website, but before they do that, they want to have the perfect logo. Once they've got that, they want to figure out the perfect color scheme. Once they've got that, they want to find the perfect developer. Then they want the whole thing, every detail, to be custom-built.

They want all this stuff for their business in place before they even sell a single product, and they don't realize that by focusing on all these things, they are jeopardizing their chance for success. All of this stuff might have to be put in place at some point to make your business extremely good, but if you stare at all the things that need to be done in the beginning, you're hurting yourself. Your brain is just going to say, "It's not worth it. I don't know how to do all of that."

The massive task of building a successful and sustainable business has to be accomplished in chunks. Your brain can handle doing a few things to make your business better every day, without any issues whatsoever, for years on end. So, the key is to keep giving yourself small daily tasks that actually keep the needle moving forward.

It's good to have an overall master plan, but beyond that, especially if you're just starting out, just do something, *anything*. Get something out there with your stamp on it. Complexity and confusion disappear when you start working, not when you start thinking.

If you have an idea, don't allow yourself to talk yourself out of it. In the future, you can improve on what you have. You don't have to go from point A to point Z in one shot. You can go from point A to point B to point C, etc.

Once you reach a different point on your timeline, you will have much more knowledge, and you will have much more opportunity to meet and network with people who have the knowledge you now need, because you will have something to show for yourself. When you've got something to show others, that means you also have experiential knowledge to share with them.

A big problem with education today is it focuses way too much on memorization and fact-based knowledge. Experiential knowledge is way more practical and valuable in business. That's why a lot of the most successful people in the world didn't even finish college. They were out there doing and creating, and this gave them a huge edge on people who have a lot of head knowledge but no experience.

Every single day I receive hundreds of messages from people who ask me, "How do I get started?"

I answer every single one of these messages the same way: "Get started." If you want to get started in e-commerce, for example, open up a Shopify account, create an ad for a product—do something! Stop thinking about it so much. You're not going to create a perfect plan by thinking and not doing. As an entrepreneur, you always want to be in the action-taker mindset. If it's not perfection paralysis that's stopping you, the other big roadblock is often information-overload paralysis.

You might have a huge list of things to do, and when you look at that list, it makes you so overwhelmed, you don't know where to start, so you don't start at all. But if you did, you'd get things moving, and you would soon reach the end of your to-do list. Just like Newton's first law that states an object in motion stays in motion, if you start moving towards a goal, you will keep moving towards it until you reach it.

Movement opens up the doors to an infinite amount of possibilities you could not conceive of without it. Let's say you decide to get into e-commerce, and you take action. You setup your Shopify store, and then, while you're researching different ways to market your store, you come across something that sparks your interest.

So, you decide to do some research, and you land on somebody's YouTube channel that introduces you to all kinds of new business opportunities you have never heard of. One of them sounds like it would be especially relevant to your general interests, so you decide you are going to change what you're doing and follow that path instead.

Three years later, you're running your own advertising agency, helping other businesses make money, and doing extremely well for yourself. All because you took action and opened up a Shopify account.

This might go against all the advice you've heard, but when you're just getting started and trying to find your way in business, I encourage you to go off the deep end. Try too many things. Get in over your head. Find out what you love.

True success doesn't come from following anyone else's formula. True success comes from being true to yourself. Once you know what you want to do, I absolutely encourage you to invest in learning the winning formula for doing that thing, but until then, take action, explore, and make decisions that are aligned with your vision of your personal future.

If you don't have an existing business that you have goals and a vision for, actively engage in discovering what opportunities are out there. Then, take the actions experts tell you to take and see what happens. Go and do. Do not worry about the consequences in the beginning. Once you've found what you love, then it's time to act with laser-like focus and determination towards a single outcome. Until you've found what you love, extreme focus like this is not possible anyway.

Don't *not* start because you don't feel educated enough. You will never know it all. When you start, you will uncover your strengths and weaknesses. You will find out what you need to know, and you will discover what you value. This will help you realize what kind of business you should create, and it will give you a clearer picture of the person you need to become to make that happen.

100

You must do something, figure out what is not going to work for you and what is going to work for you, and then run in the direction of what is working. For example, I could have put off writing this book indefinitely. I could have said, "I don't think I'm ready. Maybe in a few years I will be, but not now." I could have thrown out all my ideas for it and said to myself, "Not good enough."

But that's not what I did. I got started. This book does not have to be perfect to accomplish its purpose of helping people. And each and every one of us can accomplish our purpose without perfection. Perfection is only an illusion anyway. Perfection to you may look like a complete disaster to someone else, and that's fine.

Just by creating something—a business, a book, a software, a piece of art, or a piece of music—anything that serves some purpose to other people or to yourself, you gain something very valuable in life. You gain fulfillment of your vision.

Who knows? Maybe I'll write another book after this one, and it might be better or worse. The first software I built, which I already told you about, wasn't perfect, but right now my team and I are building an even better and more powerful one that has the potential to change people's lives forever. We could not do what we're about to do in the e-commerce space if I hadn't taken that first step and put out my first software.

I'm excited to see what comes next, and not only that, I'm also excited to see how the tools my team and I create empower other people to succeed in business at a highlevel. You can never see the finish line from the starting line. But you have to run the race knowing it will be worth it to cross it.

The more you do, the more you experience, and the more you put yourself out there, the more you are allowing yourself to be changed by stimuli in the world. You might be affected by a book you read, a place you travel, great food you eat, or a social interaction you have that shifts your

101

perspective. Anything you do that offers you a new way of viewing the world can be beneficial to you in your business.

Think of two people; we'll call them John and Jack. John grew up in a small town, went to high school there, went to college in the local area, and then got a job in the same town he grew up in. He got married, had kids, and lived happily ever after. But he never chased any dreams, and he was constantly stressed about money to the point where it made him sick.

Jack grew up in the same small town, graduated high school there, and then moved to a different area to go to college. After college, he moved to a different city, and then he met somebody he fell in love with along the way who came from a very different background.

This made him more open-minded. He got a job, did some traveling, and while traveling, he saw a product that was selling well in another country and thought, "That would be great to have in America."

So, he came back to America, started importing the product and selling it, and he made more money than he ever thought possible. Then he wrote about this experience, and he was able to make a positive impact on other people in the world. As a result, he ended up doing very well financially, and he was able to leave money behind for his loved ones and the causes he cared about at the end of his life.

In everyday life, which one of these people, John or Jack, saw more opportunity? Was it John, who stayed in one place his whole life, or was it Jack, who went out and saw the world? The answer is so obvious—Jack saw more opportunity.

But how many people today recognize the importance of getting out there and experiencing the world? Yeah, we've got the internet, and we can learn about the world online. We can also learn about the world through great books. But there is no substitute for just getting out there and hunting for opportunity. Opportunity is everywhere in the real world, but a lot of times you have to be focused on finding it before it will appear to you.

For example, I visited China recently, and I stayed at some of the higher-end hotels while I was there. The first hotel I stayed in, I opened up the door to the bathroom, and the toilet seat lifted up for me all by itself. I was immediately curious about the toilet, and after looking it over, I realized it was a smart toilet with a heated seat, a sprayer that cleaned you off automatically, and a dryer. I'd never seen a toilet like it before.

The next hotel I went to, in a different part of China, also had one. By the time I left China, I never wanted to go back to using a regular toilet ever again! But while I was still there, I started asking around about these smart toilets. I learned they are prevalent in about eight percent of the high-end hotels in China.

The reason for my trip to China was to attend a big trade show to see if I could find a product I could bring back to America to sell. Well, the best thing I found was right there in my hotel bathroom—the smart toilet. So, at the trade show, I found about forty different smart toilet manufacturers, and I talked to all of them until I found one who could make them for a fraction of the price most of the manufacturers quoted me.

When I got home, I did some research and found out there is only one brand selling smart toilets in the United States, and they're not selling a ton of them yet. Also, they're selling them for almost $10,000. Most companies and individuals are not going to spend that much on a toilet, but at the price I found them for, I can sell them for much less.

Once I saw this, the deal was done in my mind. I decided to take action and make my own smart toilet brand. Now, remember, this isn't my first time doing something like this, so I was able to go from idea to product very quickly. I called up my brand designer and my web developer, and I got my smart toilet brand ready to hit the market within a day. I've already had success selling these toilets to a luxury apartment complex here in Florida, and I expect many more deals to come.

Here's the important thing I want you to take away from this story. Did I ever think I was going to be selling toilets in a million years? Absolutely not. But by getting out there, *doing*, and looking for opportunity, I found a way to make great money, bring an awesome product to a different part of the world, and have fun doing it!

All this came about because I was out there taking action and looking at things from different angles. When I saw the opportunity, I didn't get overwhelmed. I simply followed the steps I've taken before. I knew I could make this work because I've done things like it before so many times. I know the process now, only because I've taken action in the past.

That's the importance of doing things. It always prepares you for the future, even if you fail. It's tempting to sit back and watch the world go by, but as human beings, we have the ability to change the world around us.

If I had never traveled to China or started a business before, I might have gone to China, seen the exact same toilets and said, "Oh, these are cool." That would have been the end of it. But since I've trained myself to see opportunity in the world around me, that was not the case. This is the major difference between entrepreneurs and everybody else. Most people, if they want to make some money, just go looking for a job. But the entrepreneur knows if he wants to make money, he should go looking for opportunity.

Learning how to see opportunity requires facing your fears, traveling, creating, taking notes on what you've learned, and always thinking about how to make things better. The world does not have to remain the same as it has always been. *You have the power to shape it.*

When I was working as the marketing director for a social media company, I got the opportunity to travel all over the world and stay in different places for over a month at a time. I went to New Zealand, Australia, England, and Ireland. My job was to find college students and get them interested in using our app.

To accomplish this, I had to immerse myself in all the different cultures, find out what the students liked, where they liked to hang out, and who the influential people were on campus. I spent a year and a half of my life doing this, and I learned so much about myself and the world around me. Every experience I had added a different perspective to my view of life.

The more you are able to look at the world from different perspectives, the more opportunity you are able to see. The more opportunity you are able to see, the greater impact you are able to make on the world around you. But to make an impact, you have to act. Get started!

Chapter 10

You Will Find It

When you see people like Elon Musk, who just keeps crushing it with companies like Tesla and SpaceX, it's only natural to think, "Man, how does he do that?" The guy sold $3.5 million worth of "fake" flamethrowers in five days. Prior to that, he made $1 million selling hats to raise money for his business instead of taking on investors.

People familiar with Musk's reputation probably saw this stuff happen and thought, "Yeah, that's what I would expect from him."

Other people probably saw what happened and thought, "Why do people who are already super successful always keep winning?" Well, there is actually a reason why this happens. But first, there's something else you have to understand.

Super-successful people always seem to win because their wins are always way bigger than their failures. Their failures go unnoticed, even failures most people would consider significant, while their successes take up the spotlight. For every one win a successful person has, they have most likely already experienced ten losses.

When it comes to my personal experience, I've had a few big wins, but I've also had over fifty losses. I've tried a lot of things that didn't work. The reason I don't talk about all the small failures I've experienced in detail is there is not much to say about them. I tried something; it didn't work. Every entrepreneur has experienced this.

But, with that being said, most people are probably not going to make a million dollars selling hats. So, how are people like Musk different? How do they do it?

What people don't realize is people like Musk are not superhuman. Don't get me wrong. Musk is a very smart guy. But that's not necessarily where his ability to sell twenty thousand flame throwers in five days comes from. Instead, it comes from his superhuman belief in himself based on having already succeeded at an extremely highlevel. The big wins he's already had have allowed him to develop certainty that his ideas are going to work, and that's what really makes the difference.

Now, if you haven't experienced any big wins for yourself, but you're aiming for one, you have to do something to build up your belief in yourself. You have to sell yourself on the fact that if you take the necessary action, you're going to get the result you're after. But when someone has already achieved a lot, or they know for certain things can and will work out for them, this has a direct effect on the outcome they experience.

It's totally normal to feel inferior to someone who has accomplished much more than you have. That's natural. But, to get around this feeling of inferiority and develop confidence in your own ability, you have to realize the only thing that separates the people at the top from those who want to be there is the people at the top have put in the work, doubted themselves, dealt with the stress, and thought about quitting at some point, just like you.

The difference? They didn't quit. They kept going. They continued to build their network. And they learned along the way that if you do the work required to put the right pieces into place, success doesn't get handed to you like a winning lottery ticket. It's earned.

If you are doubting yourself, I want you to know you can win if you put the right pieces into place. To do this, you have to put in the proper effort, build the proper team around you, and use the proper strategy. When you do these things, success is guaranteed to happen. Certainty comes from perseverance and realizing there is always a solution to any problem you might face, and as long as you don't quit, *you will find it.*

When I first got started in business, I looked up to everyone. If I met someone who had done anything in business, my first thought was, "My God, I need to get to know this person and learn from them." This served me well in the beginning. It's good to have people you look up to, but there are two levels to this.

Level one is full of people who have done more than you. When you're first getting started, that's pretty much anyone who already has a business. You want to absorb all the knowledge you can from these people, but don't pick up their bad habits or patterns by accident, thinking you're doing the right things.

There were a lot of people I looked up to when I started out as an entrepreneur. For example, when I first started out in the event space, there was a guy who lived near me that had a concert promotion business. I thought he was awesome because he would do concerts every month and bring in a thousand people to each one. I thought that was insane back then.

But now, looking back, I've realized this guy was just repeating the same pattern over and over again. He'd get the exact same artists or the same caliber of artists for every show, and every show brought in the same amount of people. Every show was in the same city. He didn't even try to grow. He didn't push himself. He just got to the level he was at, and that was it for him. He never broke past that barrier.

I learned what I could by observing this guy, and two years later, when I was running my own concert promotion company, I started doing five-thousand-person concerts every month in different cities. At that point, there was nothing more for me to learn from him. He did have an influence on me, but it was relatively short-lived.

The second level of people are the people at the very top. These are world-class mentors who you may not have access to, but they still inspire you and show you what's possible. For me, in this class of people, I put Mark Cuban. I've always looked up to him because of all the things he's done and accomplished.

This second level of role models is not just great to have when you have outgrown people in level one; they are also great to have when you are just getting started. These kinds of people, just by existing, will help you expand your vision. They will keep you pushing and reaching for more. If you can visualize greater success in your future, you can keep yourself on the right track moving towards it.

Visualization is something everybody, from the beginner to the seasoned entrepreneur, must take advantage of. When you have great role models, people who are just above where you are, and people who are living on the furthest edge of what's possible, they can help you visualize your future.

I've done exercises where I've visualized every aspect of my life and what I want to happen in the future. It's important to create this picture in your mind. Because if you don't know what you want, then you won't know what decisions to make. As you live and gain more experience in life, what you want will change, but it should only change in ways that are positive, and not because you have decided to settle for less.

There are so many people trying to influence us every single day of our lives. Most people allow themselves to be influenced mostly by other people and never realize they have the ability to influence themselves directly. When you decide to take control, you can literally determine the direction of your future.

In 2017, when I attended a Tony Robbins' event called "Unleash the Power Within" in LA, we did a visualization exercise. The point of the exercise was to create a vision of your ideal life.

To do this exercise, you write down where you want to live, what kind of house you want to live in, what car you drive, what you want your relationships and your family to look like, and what you want to be doing every day. You also take time to write down exactly where you'd like to be in terms of your physical, financial, and spiritual health.
Then you really visualize this scenario as if you are there. You feel it, smell it, hear it, and taste it. You are there, and you imagine the details that make it real to you.

The next step is to imagine yourself living completely inside of this life you created, but then you begin getting pulled away. You start losing the success you just visualized. You start disappointing your family and become someone bad. You begin failing over and over again, and it's because you're cheating yourself. You're not committed. You're out of shape physically, financially, and spiritually. You're getting older. You aren't sure if you can trust the people around you. Your relationships are strained. And you're moving further and further away from your ideal life every day.

When we went through this part of the exercise at the event, it lasted for about ten minutes, and it was extremely painful and horrible. It is difficult to deeply imagine losing all you care about and hope for in life. But there is a psychological reason to go through this process.

During this step of losing a grip on your dream life, you are to imagine two huge rubber bands attached to your back. As you move in the wrong direction, away from your vision, these rubber bands are stretching further and further. Finally, they stretch to their max and quickly snap back in the opposite direction. This causes them to fling you at top speed towards the vision you created of your ideal life.

This mental exercise is very powerful because it helps you define what you want out of life, and by imagining what it would be like to lose that, you become emotionally connected to what you want. When the picture of what's possible for you is real in your mind, you are much more likely to stay to committed to your vision. This is how our brains work. We will work much harder to keep something we already have than to get something we don't already have.

Here's another exercise we did that helped me a lot. Once you have the complete picture of your dream life created, imagine you are someone else in your life that you know loves you, cares about you, and wants the best for you. This could be a family member, a friend, or anyone you know who has always had your best interest in mind. For example, the person I imagined when doing this exercise was my aunt. She's always been a very positive influence in my life.

Now, imagine you are seeing the world through this person's eyes, and imagine you are walking up the driveway to your dream house. From this person's perspective, you see your dream car parked in the garage, and you're genuinely happy for you.

Now you walk into the house and start looking around. It's a beautiful place, the kind of home people dream about owning. You look around, and there are pictures on the walls of your family, all smiling together.

You continue walking around the house and admiring all the nice features, and then you head into bathroom. You look into the mirror, and your perspective shifts from that of

111

your loved one, to your own. You realize you are you, and this whole time you were feeling genuinely happy for yourself and proud of yourself. You love your life!

I absolutely love this exercise and encourage you to practice it for yourself, because so often we are ridiculously hard on ourselves. We might be crushing it in business, taking care of our loved ones and friends, and making a positive impact on the world, but still not feeling happy about what we've accomplished. We don't feel proud of ourselves, and we think we will love our lives eventually, someday.

But by putting yourself into the shoes of someone that you know loves you, is proud of you, and cares about you, you allow yourself to feel those feelings for yourself. This is an extremely positive emotional experience we rarely give ourselves, but it can totally change the way you view your life.

I truly believe going through this visualization exercise can bring about a huge breakthrough for you. It could be the thing that takes you from thinking the vision you have for your life could be possible, to *knowing* it is possible and knowing exactly what to do to make it real.

It is amazing how powerful connecting your emotions to your goals through visualization can be. It allows you to unlock an enormous amount of your potential that otherwise might take a long time to come to the surface. As human beings, we are more than just our ability to think and plan. Deep inside, it is our emotions that do most of the heavy lifting in our lives, and they can do it quickly.

After doing both of the exercises I just explained to you in detail, I was able to use both my emotions and my intellect to take my business to a whole new level. The very next day, I was operating on a whole new creative level as I drove from the "Unleash the Power Within" event in LA to my new home in Florida. Because of that, I was able to take my online store from zero to $2 million in sixty days. Five months after that, I had the exact car I had visualized sitting in my driveway.

This might sound like magic to most people, and at first, I thought so too. But the truth is every single one of us has an enormous amount of potential lying dormant inside of us, just waiting for us to start engaging with it and letting it out into the world. Through visualization, you can connect with this potential that is already there, and start pulling it out and putting it to use in your life, just as I did when I scaled my store rapidly.

If you've been working hard for years, but feel something is holding you back, or if you are just now getting serious about going after the life of your dreams, I highly recommend you *start practicing visualization.* It can help you integrate all the different parts of yourself, tap into your potential, and set you on the right path to obtaining the life you have always wanted.

Chapter 11

The Road to Power

You have now come to the final chapter of this book. I hope you've gained a lot of valuable insight you can take with you and use to produce massive success in your own life. What I've shared with you comes from my own personal experience, based on what I wish I knew years ago about what it takes to succeed in life and in business.

There is no doubt that when you put what you've learned in this book into practice, the results you get will be different than my own, even if you follow my advice to the letter. But this is good!

Unlocking your own true potential is the only way to succeed at the highest level. There is no fulfillment to be found in trying to live according to someone else's version of success. True success is something only you can define, and even then, life has a funny way of blowing your highest expectations out of the water. I am confident that on your journey, you will have many amazing experiences you never could have predicted. I know I have.

For example, about a year ago I moved into the neighborhood I currently live in here in Florida. I've got a great house here on a golf course with a green just outside my back door. Since moving here, I've gotten more serious about my golf game and have enjoyed my time out on the course.

My neighbors here are awesome and very friendly. One gentleman I've gotten to know very well is a criminal attorney toward the end of his career. He has shared with me a lot of life wisdom and introduced me to some incredible people.

One day, he invited me to go play golf with him in Jupiter, Florida, at one of the most exclusive country club golf courses in the United States called The Bear's Club. Through one of his connections, he managed to get us a tee time there on an absolutely beautiful day.

To start, we decided to hit some practice shots at the driving range. When we got there, one of the best golfers in the world, Rory McIlroy, was also there hitting balls. That alone would have been enough to make my day great, but even more excitement was coming.

After warming up a bit, we got out on the course, and the weather was perfect. We had an awesome caddie, and we both enjoyed playing a fantastic round of golf. When we finished up, I noticed I had two missed calls on my phone, both from my neighbor's wife. I knew my neighbor hadn't had cell phone service on the course all day, so I called her back immediately to see what was going on.

When she picked up, she said, "Jared, MJ's mother-in-law said you guys can go see his house if you want to. I need to let her know right now, though, if you're going to go."

Yeah, that MJ—Michael Jordan. The greatest basketball player to ever play the game. My neighbor had once casually told me he was friends with Jordan, but I wasn't expecting this. Of course, I wanted to go!

It took us a long time to find Jordan's house because the address we had was just a number. There were no street names in this exclusive community. After looking for it for about ten minutes, we finally spotted it and pulled into the driveway. Now, I say driveway, but it was more like a parking lot for the 40,000- square foot mansion that stood behind it.

Once we parked, two security guards approached the car. "Gentlemen, this way," they said, and we followed them up to the house. At this point, I still couldn't believe I was about to walk into Michael Jordan's house.

We stepped through the door, and then the security guards guided us through the massive house and towards the backyard. As we were walking through, I spotted Jordan outside. In my head, I thought, "No way! This is impossible. This is insane!"

I thought we were just going to take a tour of the house and then leave. I didn't actually expect Jordan to be there. But there he was, the GOAT, in the flesh. It's not every day you get invited to meet a living legend in their own backyard.

When we stepped outside, I was introduced to Jordan, and we shook hands. I couldn't believe I was face-to-face with one of the greatest athletes on the face of this earth. Before I knew it, we were all sitting there in his backyard smoking Cuban cigars and sipping a $5,000 bottle of tequila. Then my neighbor asked Jordan, "Would you be down to show Jared your trophy room?"

The next thing I knew, I was standing in the middle of Jordan's personal trophy room. The ceiling was composed of the old floor of the Bulls' Chicago Stadium. Jordan went through all the trophies and awards he had stored in there, including some fun pop-culture stuff like his personal Wheaties box and photos. As he went through each item, he told me stories about all of his experiences in basketball and in life.

As I stood there listening to none other than Michael Jordan tell me about how he had pushed himself to succeed at such a highlevel throughout his career, I couldn't help but ask myself, "How did I end up here? How in the world did this happen?"

People would literally hop on a plane and fly across the world at a moment's notice to get a tour of Jordan's house, trophies, and memorabilia from the man himself, and yet here I was in the middle of such a tour, by chance, one afternoon after a round of golf with a friend. I realized right then there was no way I could have predicted this would happen. And I also couldn't have predicted how excited and motivated I felt after leaving Jordan's house that day. It was a fantastic reminder of the great rewards that come from pushing yourself to reach your full potential in life and everything you do.

I share this story with you because it's a great example of how surprising and exciting life can be. It's impossible to predict where you will end up. But when you create an incredible vision for your future, and you have the courage to go after it with all your heart, the results of doing so are incredible. When you open up to the possibilities in your life, the possibilities open up to you.

There are infinite opportunities to learn and grow every day, and most of the time these opportunities come at times you would not expect. For example, I was recently boarding a flight from New York back to my home in Florida. As I got on the plane, I noticed an older lady who looked like she needed some help getting her bags loaded up, so I offered her a hand.

As fate would have it, we actually ended up sitting right next to each other on the flight. She was a sweet old lady, and after I had helped her out, she started talking to me a lot. She asked me all kinds of questions about myself and started telling me stories about herself and her family.

At first, I was kind of hoping she would stop talking so I could go to sleep or read the book I had with me. I was kind of tired from my trip, and I didn't feel like talking the whole flight. However, it became clear she was in the mood to talk, so I told myself, "Jared, why don't you just be nice and see if you can keep up a good conversation for this whole flight? Maybe you'll learn something."

So, I made it my goal to listen to what this woman had to say for the rest of the flight, and to see what I could learn from her. What I learned was she had been married for fifty years, and her husband was there on the plane with us as well. I asked them both all kinds of questions about their lives, and I found out they were in their seventies and eighties.

After we had talked for a while, I learned they had done a lot of traveling together over the years, and it was clear they were very happy people. So, I finally asked them the big question, "What's made you the happiest in life?"

The woman thought for a moment, and then responded, "The thing that's made me the happiest in my life was spending time with my parents before they passed away."

It was such a simple answer from someone who had clearly achieved a lot and had a very successful and happy marriage for fifty years. I realized then that often the best answers to the big questions in life are extremely simple, and her response made me think about my own life.

Oftentimes, as entrepreneurs, we become so focused on growth and progress that we forget to enjoy the amazing things we have around us right now. For this woman, one of her gifts in life was her relationship with her parents. Not everyone can say that, but everyone has someone or something in their life that is very important to them. Making time for these people and these things is critical for long-lasting happiness.

My own life can be very busy. I travel all the time. I live in Florida, and my mom lives in New York. It can be challenging to find time to connect with her, but I learned on this flight how important finding the time to connect with loved ones truly is.

I didn't anticipate having a conversation like that when I hopped on the flight back home, but its effect on my state of mind was profound. I started thinking about all the different relationships in my life and how important they are to me. And it's not just romantic relationships or family relationships that are important.

In fact, a lot of people don't realize this, but business, too, is all about relationships. I used to think when it came to business, it was you versus me, and whoever got the most out of the relationship was the winner. But that attitude just made me paranoid. It made me feel like I couldn't trust people, and that if I let my guard down, I was setting myself up for failure. But as I gained more experience, I learned relationships in business are everything.

I've learned to be more open and friendly with people. I've also learned the more you can relate to the people you're working with, the better the business you can do together. You can accomplish much more with a light touch than you can with a heavy hand. And doing business is simply a lot more enjoyable when you have good relationships with the people you're working with.

For example, at the time of this writing, I'm working with a new supplier in China to prepare for the next phase of my business. In the past, when I didn't know what I know now, I would have messaged him only when I needed something or when something was going wrong which I felt I needed to step in and correct.

Instead of continuing to follow that pattern, I decided to take a different approach most inexperienced entrepreneurs don't take. I went out to China just to spend time with this supplier and his family. We ate and drank together and enjoyed each other's company. We didn't even talk business for most of the day we spent together.

Eventually, we did talk business, but before that, we simply connected as human beings. We were able to bond over shared interests and started to actually care about each other. To me, when there is mutual caring, that's the sign of a long-lasting and fruitful business relationship that has a lot of potential.

If you are constantly trying to get the upper hand in business all the time, you're going to miss out on the opportunity to actually enjoy your work, and ironically, you're going to burn more bridges to success than you build.

Sure, not everyone is going to like you, but if you're trustworthy, honest, and caring, your network will expand like crazy. The compounding effect of being a good person and being willing to see the value in other people you are working with is way more beneficial than it is possible to logically calculate.

There is a competitive side to business, and this is good too. Competition makes everybody better. The irony is, if you want to beat ninety-nine percent of the competition, the best way to do that is by focusing on building good relationships with the people you want to do business with. Most people are only focused on themselves, but doing good business is all about aligning your vision with other people's and creating win-win situations.

If you're only in business to see what you can get for yourself, that's a losing strategy. But if you can anchor what you're doing to a greater purpose outside of yourself, you will be much more likely to succeed.

No matter how disciplined you are, it's easy to make excuses for yourself and stall on projects when you can't see the consequences of doing this clearly. This is why you must know *why* you absolutely must do what you've set out to do.
Do you want to succeed to give your family a better quality of life? Do you want to change the way the world does something, and make it more efficient and sustainable? Do you want to provide people with access to awesome products they've never seen before? Do you want to help people living in poverty?

No matter what it is you're trying to accomplish in business or in your life in general, you must tie it to a bigger purpose outside of yourself. If you don't, when you are challenged, it is likely you will say to yourself, "I don't need to do this today. It can wait. I'll do it tomorrow." And you probably know by now, "I'll do it tomorrow" is the biggest lie we can tell ourselves.

Most people don't know how to strengthen their sense of internal responsibility to get something done. This is because all of our lives we are told what to do, when to do it, and what to expect when we do. Our parents, our teachers, and our society do their best to explain to us the expectations, consequences, and rewards of taking certain actions in the world.

But if you want to succeed in business for yourself, you have to learn how to define your own expectations, consequences, and rewards. These things are not a given. The best way to bring a sense of urgency and responsibility to your work is to find your greater and deeper *why*.

That might be, "I need to take care of my spouse. I need to take care of my kids. I need to take care of my parents. I need to be a role model for the young people growing up in my neighborhood." This external purpose will drive your internal purpose even deeper and allow it to grow stronger. Then, when you wake up in the morning with a full day of hard work ahead of you, you're not going to want to climb back in bed and put it off. You're going to get up ready to go because you know you can't let everyone down.

If all you want out of your business is material things, there's no doubt in my mind you can get them. But when you do, you will begin to realize you still need to answer these bigger questions, or life and business will become very unfulfilling for you.

Personal growth is not just about what you have done, what you are going to do, or what you need to do right now. It's about learning to become increasingly grateful for everything in your life. If you're not grateful for your relationships, for the material things you possess, for your own skills, and for everything you've learned in life so far, then you are creating resentment. You're telling yourself nothing is good enough, and if you make that a habit, even if you have everything, you will not be happy.

Don't get this backwards. More good things in your life will not produce more gratitude. *More gratitude produces more good things in your life.* Gratitude is a feeling you can feel, no matter what your present situation. You can feel grateful for something so simple as the ability to breathe. You can feel grateful for the ability to read this book.

No matter who you are, there are so many things you *can* do. Don't spoil your happiness by focusing on all the things you *can't* do *yet*. Your time will come, and when it does, if you have been practicing gratitude for some time, it will be all the more fulfilling.

I start every single day in gratitude because I want to set up the right conditions for myself to be able to enjoy whatever happens in my life each day. When I meditate or when I'm exercising, I often think about people and experiences I've had in my life that I'm grateful for. These aren't all people or experiences that are in my life right now, but I still value them.

For example, four years ago, my Nani, who I had a extraordinary bond with, passed away. This was a woman who I loved as much or more than anyone in the world. Our connection was indescribable, and I never thought I would lose her so early.

But there are two ways I can choose to look at this situation. I can think about how unfair it was that she died and how I wish she was still around to share her wisdom and insight with me. Or I can think about how grateful I am to have had her in my life for as long as I did because she loved me unconditionally, and she made me feel valued, like I was truly a special person.

If I didn't look at this experience of losing someone important to me with gratitude, what was a great relationship with another human being in the past would only drag me down in the present. But because I look at it with gratitude, it provides me with strength and energy to live my life today. That's the power of gratitude. When frustrations and problems pop up, gratitude brings you back to the present moment and allows you to be thankful for it.

There are times when I look at the numbers in my businesses, and it can be tempting to focus on all the expenses. This is a perfect example of the power of your perspective. In reality, the expenses produce the profit in my businesses. But, just by staring at them and not the overall result, I catch myself sometimes feeling broke, even when that's nowhere near the truth.

This is why I've trained myself to change perspective when I notice negative thinking starting to creep in. I change my perspective by thinking about all the great things I have in my life. I have a wonderful, supportive, loving relationship with my girlfriend. I live in a great house. I have my dream cars. I have an incredible team beside me. By focusing on all these positive things, I can shift my mindset to a state of gratitude within seconds. And with this perspective driving my actions, I can make every day of my life the best day possible.

You have this power too. You have a choice about which perspective you are going to take every moment of your life. You are in control of your thoughts and how you direct them. You're the only one that can change things if they aren't going your way. You are the only one you need to hold accountable for absolutely everything.

Will Smith did a video on this concept you can find on YouTube. In it, he said, "Your heart, your life, your happiness— is your responsibility and your responsibility alone...*the road to power is in taking responsibility.*"

Taking responsibility for your life is not a one-time action. You may have decided you're going to make some changes based on the things you've learned in this book, and you may have already made them. If that's the case, I congratulate you. You have recognized the most important thing you have to do in order to succeed in any area of life, and that is you have to take personal responsibility for everything.

But the key is you can't just do this once in your life and expect a miracle shift to occur. Taking responsibility for your life, its direction, and the impact you are making on the world around you is an active, daily practice. You have to do it over and over again, even when you can't see the benefits. Even when it would be a lot easier to blame someone or something else for whatever is going on.

I believe there is enormous power and potential inside of you that's just waiting to be released in your life. But you have to claim it. You have to take responsibility for it, and along with that, you have to take responsibility for breaking past all the things that may be holding you back from experiencing success in life beyond your wildest imagination.

This may sound like a daunting task, but if I can go from rock bottom at age twenty-two, to enjoying greater success and fulfillment in life and business than I ever thought possible at age twenty-eight, just imagine what kind of a journey you might have ahead of you. No one can predict the future, but if you're willing to take responsibility for it, no matter what, I can guarantee things are going to work out for you, even better than you expect them to.